IMAGES
of America

FORT
LESLEY J. MCNAIR

MAP
of the
CITY OF WASHINGTON

PUBLISHED BY W.ᴹ M.MORRISON, 1846.

This 1846 map of Washington, DC, shows the initial impact of Pierre L'Enfant's plan with modifications by Andrew Ellicott. It would not be until the 1900s, when the McMillan plan was implemented, that L'Enfant's initial sweeping mall and other additions would be enacted. Meanwhile, Greenleaf Point became Washington Arsenal and would be soon serving the Union's needs in the Civil War. (Library of Congress.)

ON THE COVER: Fort Lesley J. McNair, known during the Civil War as Washington Arsenal, was one of two arsenals provisioning the Union troops during the conflict. This row of smoothbore, Napoleon-style artillery was captured at the Confederate Arsenal in Richmond, Virginia, after the US Civil War. In the background is a soldier on his horse. Behind him is the model arsenal, a building that still stands today as Davis Hall. The Lincoln assassination conspirators were hanged nearby. (Library of Congress.)

IMAGES
of America

FORT
LESLEY J. MCNAIR

John Michael

ARCADIA
PUBLISHING

Published by Arcadia Publishing
Charleston, South Carolina

Library of Congress Control Number: 2014950954

For all general information, please contact Arcadia Publishing:
Telephone 843-853-2070
Fax 843-853-0044
E-mail sales@arcadiapublishing.com
For customer service and orders:
Toll-Free 1-888-313-2665

Visit us on the Internet at www.arcadiapublishing.com

This book is dedicated to Mr. Kim Bernard Holien. It is also dedicated to those who walk, study, and work among the acres of the post and all those who have done the same over time. Thank you for your service.

CONTENTS

ACKNOWLEDGMENTS

One name appears on the cover of this book; however, it took a team of people who were involved in the actual production of this work. Since this is my second project with Arcadia (the first being Images of America: *Fort Myer*), the core team from the first book was excited for the challenge ahead. Special thanks go out to Kim Bernard Holien for his continued guidance and the great resources that were made available from the Mr. Kim Bernard Holien Historical Collection, now within the Special Collections of the National Defense University. Thanks also to special collections librarian Susan Lemke and Abigail Gardner for allowing me access to the collection.

To the Library of Congress, thank you for making your images so easily searchable and accessible. To Holly Reed and Theresa Roy and the staff at the National Archives in College Park, Maryland— thank you for reorienting me to the collections, and thank you especially to Theresa for helping me obtain an image of L'Enfant! It was Brig. Gen. Tom Consentino, commandant of the National War College, who was kind enough to provide a personal tour of historic Roosevelt Hall. Thanks to M.Sgt. Dean Welch, Department of the Army, Office of Public Affairs. A special thanks to Adrienne Combs, deputy director of Public Affairs, Military District of Washington, for connecting me with the Office of Public Affairs. Also a special thanks to Leah Rubicalah and Courtney Dock, both of the Public Affairs Office of Fort Myer–Henderson Hall for providing assistance in the capture of the present-day photographs of Fort Lesley J. McNair. To two of my advisors/ mentors—Lt. Col. William Lee Yarborough, USA (Ret.), and Lt. Col. Wallace Johnson, USA (Ret.)—thank you for your guidance, insights, and encouragements over the years. I would have never reached this point without you. Thanks also to Col. John H. Crerar, USA (Ret.), and Dr. Virginia Norton, whose proofreading skills provided major improvements to my wordsmithing. To my editor, Gillian Nicol, thank you for the major role of making sure we were going to get this done; with your help, we did!

Images in this volume appear courtesy of US National Archives and Records Administration (NARA), US Library of Congress (LOC), Mr. Kim Bernard Holien Historical Collection (KBH), and the US Army (USA). A special thank you to Angela Ponte and Carol Pollard for use of their photographs of Gen. Lesley J. McNair's grave marker at the Normandy Cemetery in Normandy, France.

INTRODUCTION

If you ask a native Washingtonian about Fort Lesley J. McNair, unless they are military or are associated with the federal government, the answer would probably be a blank stare. With a current land area of less than 100 acres, this iconic US Army post is nestled away in the southwest part of Washington, DC. As the third-oldest continuously operating post (West Point and Carlisle Barracks are older), it is one of the most beautiful US Army installations, with a great complement of historic buildings. It has no ranges or place to hold maneuvers. It currently garrisons no troops—the 3rd Infantry ("the Old Guard"/Alpha Company/Commander-in-Chief's Guard)—was located on post a few years ago until the company was relocated to barracks on Fort Myer, Virginia.

The headquarters of the Military District of Washington has been located on post along with the Center of Military History, which also shares Fort McNair. Among the educational entities on post is the Industrial College of the Armed Forces (ICAF), now known as the Dwight D. Eisenhower School for National Security and Resource Strategy, which has been there since 1962. The primary "resident" of the post is the National Defense University, along with several of its colleges—National War College at Roosevelt Hall being the primary. Roosevelt Hall—the iconic building within Fort Lesley J. McNair—is named for Theodore "Teddy" Roosevelt, who, along with secretary of war Elihu Root, conceived of the need for a place to educate the US military. It was designed by the firm of McKim, Mead & White, and President Roosevelt laid the cornerstone in 1903. The building was completed in 1907, and it housed the US Army War College until 1946. Today, it contains the National War College.

The post also provides housing for senior military officers among the historic Generals' Row of century-plus-old housing built when the engineering school was at Washington Barracks (a previous name for Fort McNair).

Over time, the acreage had increased to just over 100 acres—the initial expanse was barely 28. Through the years, the post has been home to the US Army Music School, the US Army Engineering School, the US Army Band ("Pershing's Own"), and the US Army War College. It has only been invaded once, during the British invasion of Washington during the War of 1812. British casualties occurred when the gunpowder stored down a dry well exploded, taking the lives of nearly two dozen Royal Marines. Another explosion occurred some 50 years later in June 1864, killing 21 women arsenal workers who were working at the table where the gunpowder exploded. Their funeral service began at the Washington Arsenal and then proceeded to Congressional Cemetery, with President Lincoln leading the procession.

When Lincoln was assassinated, the conspirators were first incarcerated aboard ironclad boats moored in the river; they were later held in the DC federal penitentiary on the north end of the peninsula. Their incarceration would last seven weeks while they were tried on the third floor of an adjoining building. More than 370 witnesses appeared before the military commission, which would find four of the conspirators guilty. The four were hanged on July 7, 1865, and Mary Surratt became the first American woman hanged by the federal government to die on the gallows.

Maj. Walter Reed was assigned to the 7th Field Artillery at Washington Barracks in 1882. His assignment here allowed him to determine that infectious diseases such as yellow fever were carried and transmitted by the mosquito. He came to this conclusion by observing the marshy areas and the stagnant waters of James Creek to the east of then Washington Barracks. When the US Army Engineering School moved from New York to Washington Barracks, it was a time of significant construction. Nearly 50 new buildings were erected in less than 10 years. The new buildings were from the officers' club to the entire stretch of "Generals' Row" houses, complemented by a row of duplexes for noncommissioned officers (NCOs) on the east side of the parade field, two barracks for the soldiers, a stable, commissary, and the crowning jewel at the south end of the post—Roosevelt Hall, designed by the architectural firm of McKim, Mead & White. The entire post is built on swampy land and, given its location at the confluence of two rivers, is prone to flooding. Two major floods from an overabundance of rain attacked the post in 1936 and 1942. Flooding continues even today when the Potomac River rises.

The US Army Signal Corps Film Service had processing and storage facilities on post and contained Allied Expeditionary Forces (AEF) films from World War I. They were training films for the Army War College. The highly combustible films were later transferred to the National Archives in Suitland, Maryland, where, in 1978, a couple of fires in the vaults destroyed many of them. After the war, the movie *His Greatest Gift* was filmed in 1918 on what was then Washington Barracks. Soldiers garrisoned on post were included in the movie, and trenches were dug on post to provide battlefield simulation for the project.

In 1929, a nine-hole golf course was carefully placed within the acreage to provide some on-post diversion for the local residents. One of the stables was converted into the post's movie theater. Finally, in 1948, the post received its current name of Fort Lesley J. McNair, honoring Lieutenant General McNair, who was killed in action at Normandy in World War II.

In 1791, when he laid out America's new capital, Maj. Pierre Charles L'Enfant could not see two centuries ahead to predict what would become of his "military reservation #5." Through the passage of time, it has been known as Washington Barracks and Washington Arsenal, housed Washington Penitentiary, Fort Humphreys, and Army War College, and finally come to be known as Fort Lesley J. McNair.

At Fort McNair today, history is being made by the men and women who are attending National Defense University and its colleges. The movement began over a century ago with the establishment of the US Army War College within Roosevelt Hall. However, when it was first established, its role was to defend the new capital. Maj. Pierre Charles L'Enfant served in the Revolutionary War and was on Gen. George Washington's staff as an engineer. Born in Paris, France, he came to the aid of the Americans in their fight for freedom. After the war, he established a civil engineering firm in New York City. One of his first accomplishments was the redesign of the city hall of New York.

The Residence Act of July 16, 1790, as amended March 3, 1791, authorized Pres. George Washington to select a 100-square-mile site for the national capital on the Potomac River between Alexandria, Virginia, and Williamsport, Maryland. The decision was made in January 1791 by Washington, and in the same month, he appointed a commission of three to superintend the building of the federal city: Daniel Carroll (a signer of the Declaration of Independence and brother to Bishop John Carroll), Thomas Johnson, and David Stuart.

Maj. Andrew Ellicott, a surveyor from Pennsylvania, was charged with marking the perimeter of the city. He enlisted Benjamin Banneker, an astronomer and mathematician, to determine where to place the first stone marking the southernmost point of the perimeter. Banneker used the stars above, lying on his back and watching them move them across the sky, to offer a suggestion of where to place the stone. Andrew Ellicott spent the next two years surveying and placing 40 boundary stones—16 on the Virginia side and 24 on the Maryland side.

When it had been decided to place the new capital in between Maryland and Virginia, Major L'Enfant approached Washington and offered to design the layout of the city. Washington approved, and in 1791, the land on the Maryland side of the Potomac was mapped and the plan made. L'Enfant's plan called for a design that most conservative Americans thought too grandiose, and his insistence was something that the commission and Washington did not tolerate: they relieved him. The project was then assigned to Andrew Ellicott, who, along with his brother Joseph, modified L'Enfant's plan. Their modifications had no effect on Military Reservation No. 5—where L'Enfant had left a single artillery piece behind an earthworks to warn of an attack by water.

The location first became Washington Arsenal. It was at the junction of the Potomac and Anacostia Rivers—a perfect spot from which to defend against attacks by water, because ships ruled the waterways and attacks were prevalent. A small parcel of land, barely 28 acres, the peninsula was first known as Turkey Buzzard Point. It was fortunate that one of the real estate investors, James Greenleaf, quickly changed its name to Greenleaf Point. His investments were adjacent to the point and were, he thought, the most likely to make a healthy return. As the development of the capital city was concentrated to the north, the area around Greenleaf Point and the recently renamed James Creek became a less-desirable place to live.

Encompassing over two centuries of defending Washington, DC, provisioning the Union during the Civil War, the movement of various units to and from the post, and providing for the education of military and civilians in defense, the whole history of Fort Lesley J. McNair cannot be contained in any one book. Through extensive fresh research, new images have emerged to document some of the events and persons hidden away over time. Some of those images have been included in the following pages. Yet there are more, and those photographs will appear on the companion web site set up for the book—www.Historic-FortMcNair.com—along with other complementary materials.

All efforts have been made to ensure the completeness and accuracy of what is contained in this book. However, if there are errors or omissions, the author takes full responsibility; it was not by design or intent, but by being human.

Special Note: Several among the network of contacts have suggested that the post is haunted, perhaps by the ghost of Mary Surratt or maybe the ghost of Maj. Walter Reed. Many who suggested the haunting were soldiers from the 3rd Infantry who had lived on Fort McNair had experiences that they insist are the hauntings of ghosts. This needs to be substantiated, and it is left up to the readers to explore the post and seek these "haunting experiences" on their own.

The strip of land first known as Turkey Buzzard Point, then Greenleaf Point, has been called many things over the last two centuries. It began when Maj. Charles Pierre L'Enfant designed the plan for Washington, DC, and the current name happened after World War II. The listing below summarizes the name changes:

YEARS	NAME
1791–1802	Military Reservation No. 05
1803–1881	Washington Arsenal
1881–1901	Washington Barracks
1901–1935	Army War College
1935–1939	Fort Humphreys, District of Columbia
1939–1948	Army War College
1948–present	Fort Lesley J. McNair

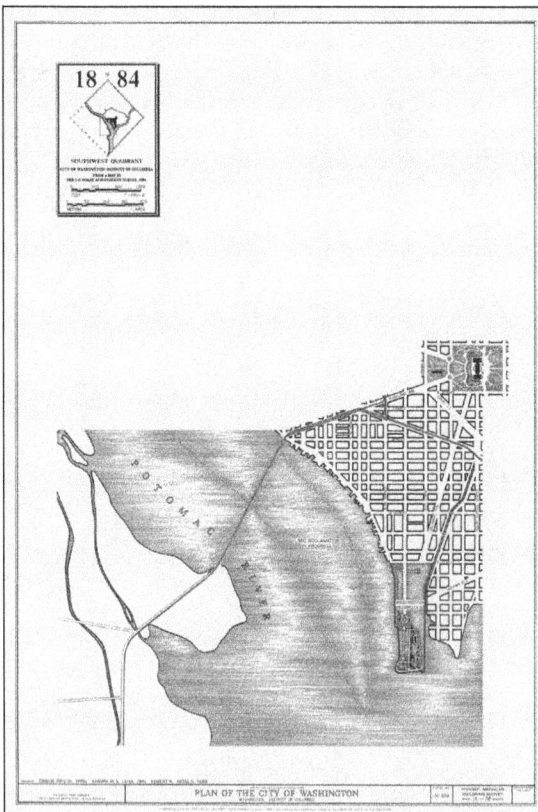

The main gate, known as the Memorial Gate, of this historic US Army post was only a single-lane entry with a railroad track that ran through post. The gateposts are six coastal defense guns, which were cast in 1850 at Tredegor Foundry in Richmond, Virginia. As the traffic created needs to expand to two lanes, the gate was maintained, and the cannon tubes were spread; they still make up the gate today. (KBH.)

This 1791 map shows a section of the new capital city of Washington, DC. It is the southwest section that includes the peninsula of approximately 28 acres then known as Turkey Buzzard Point; later, after the surrounding area was purchased by James Greenleaf, it became Greenleaf Point. (LOC.)

One

L'ENFANT HAS RESERVATIONS WITH WASHINGTON

The design and layout of Washington, DC, was a complex issue. It appears that George Washington attempted to distance himself from the actual process by setting up a commission of three men to oversee the project. He was approached by Maj. Pierre Charles L'Enfant, who wanted to design the city. L'Enfant made some bold moves in his plan based on his knowledge of many European capital cities. Sweeping, wide streets and open-air vistas would grace the new capital city. However, the Americans were much more conservative. His plan called for 17 reservations to accommodate the federal areas. Reservation No. 01 was where the president's house was to be placed, while No. 02 was where the building of Congress—the Capitol—would go. No. 03 would be where the Lincoln Memorial would be built, and No. 04 encompassed the grounds where the Washington Monument would be erected. Most interesting of all to this book is No. 05—28 acres placed at Greenleaf Point and its expansion to nearly 100 acres.

Established in 1791, the reservation later became Washington Arsenal. It initially contained a garrison of soldiers from artillery units to defend the new capital city. Artillery units were predominant residents of the acres, even though there was little room for any practical drilling of artillery.

Pres. George Washington, given the power to select the location of the new capital city, chose a 100-square-mile site on the Potomac River between Maryland and Virginia. He also chose a three-member commission to oversee the project of establishing the capital. He initially responded favorably to Maj. Pierre Charles L'Enfant request to plan and lay out the city. (LOC.)

Maj. Pierre Charles L'Enfant, who fought in the American Revolution, was an engineer born and educated in Paris, France. He was on General Washington's staff during the war. Afterward, he headed to New York, where he established his civil engineering company. He petitioned Washington to design the new capital city. Though the plans were found too grandiose, the major was insistent that it be done his way and was relieved of his duties. (NARA.)

MAJOR PIERRE CHARLES L'ENFANT
APPOINTED BY PRESIDENT WASHINGTON
TO LAY OUT THE FEDERAL CITY

On April 28, 1909, Pierre Charles L'Enfant was disinterred from Digges Farm in Prince George's County, Maryland, where he had died on June 14, 1825. A military escort transported his body to the Capitol dome on Capitol Hill. After lying in state for three hours, his body was transported by military escort to Arlington National Cemetery, where he was interred that same afternoon. The inscription on L'Enfant's grave reads, "Pierre Charles L'Enfant Engineer—Artist—Soldier under the direction of George Washington designed the plan for the federal city. Major U.S. Engineer Corps 1782. Charter member of the Society of the Cincinnati. Designed its certificate & insignia. Born in Paris, France, August 2, 1755. Died June 14, 1825 while residing at Chilham Castle Manor, Prince George's CO Maryland, and was interred there. Reinterred at Arlington April 28, 1909." (NARA.)

In 1911, on May 22, the monument marking L'Enfant's grave was dedicated, with Pres. William Howard Taft giving the dedication address. The monument itself is a marble slab held up by six posts, located at the foot of Arlington House and facing east toward the city L'Enfant designed. At the end of the marble slab is a reproduction of L'Enfant's plan as submitted to Congress in December 1791. It is a lasting tribute to the major's genius that, as the viewer stands at the foot of his grave and looks out at the city he planned over 200 years ago, the reproduction of the plan displayed on the monument can be recognized in the city across the river. L'Enfant is one of a few non–US born interred at Arlington. The above photograph—taken during the annual Memorial Day tribute, "Flags In"—displays both the US and French colors. (NARA.)

George Washington appointed three commissioners to oversee the project of the design, plan, and layout of the new capital city. They initially were: Thomas Johnson and Daniel Carroll of Maryland, and David Stuart of Virginia. James Greenleaf was born in Boston, Massachusetts, to a prominent and wealthy family. A land speculator, he was duped into marrying a Dutch nobleman's daughter when she claimed to be pregnant. His land speculation included the September 1793 purchase of 3,000 lots in the capital city; in return, he would build 10 brick houses a year for seven years and also loan the commissioners $2,660 per month. The three commissioners, in need of sales, allowed him to purchase an additional 3,000 lots in December 1793. Included in his purchase was the peninsula of land known up until then as Turkey Buzzard Point (which he renamed Greenleaf Point), upon which Military Reservation No. 5 was situated. Greenleaf built the Thomas Law House in 1795 near present-day Sixth and N Streets SW in Washington, DC. (LOC.)

Maj. Andrew Ellicott, a surveyor from Pennsylvania, was initially tasked by the three commissioners to plot and mark the boundary of the new capital city. Over a two-year period, he and Benjamin Banneker (and later, his brother Louis Ellicott) placed 40 sandstone markers—14 on the Virginia side and 26 on the Maryland side. Thanks to initial efforts by the Daughters of the Revolution, 36 of the markers are still in place today. Below is Benjamin Banneker, a black astronomer and mathematician who was hired by Andrew Ellicott to work on the project of plotting and marking the boundary of the new capital city. He used the night sky to determine where the first marker should be placed by watching the movement of the stars. He is shown here in *Benjamin Banneker: Surveyor-Inventor-Astronomer*, a mural by Maxime Seelbinder at the Recorder of Deeds building constructed in 1943 at 515 D Street NW, Washington, DC. (Both, LOC.)

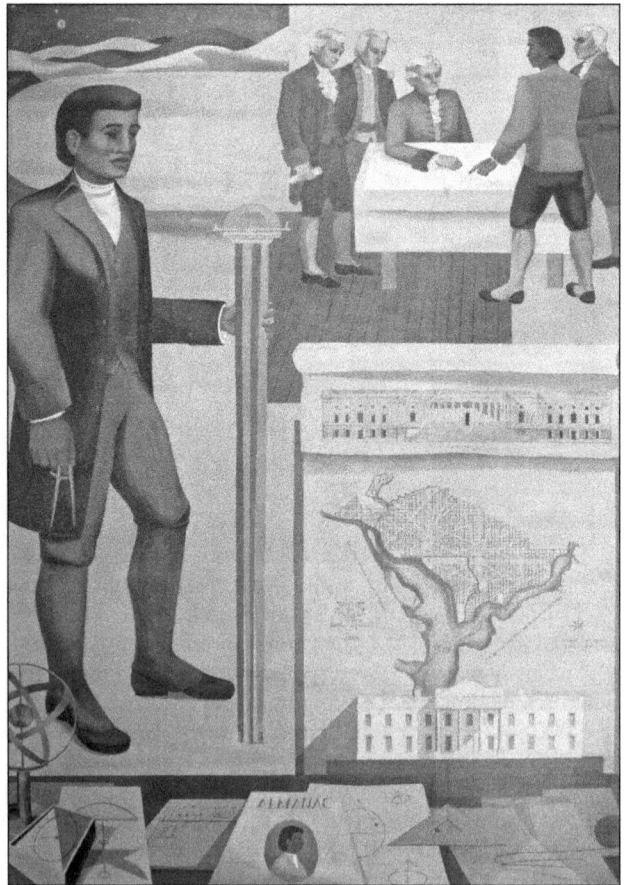

Two

THE CAPITAL NEEDS AN ARSENAL AND A PENITENTIARY

From 1803 until 1881, the acres of Fort McNair were known as Washington Arsenal. Even though there were arsenals at Harper's Ferry, West Virginia, and Springfield, Massachusetts, there was a movement and lobbying to expand the military reservation at Greenleaf Point. Buildings were constructed, and despite protests from a foundry owner in Georgetown, the arsenal operations increased. After invading British troops ransacked and burned the buildings during the War of 1812, the arsenal was rebuilt. Production included both shell and shot, and the arsenal also built and repaired gun carriages.

From 1831 to 1862, part of the northern-end acreage was devoted to the first federal penitentiary. Over protests of the War Department, sixth president John Quincy Adams authorized its construction, with architect Charles Bullfinch designing the building.

With the outbreak of the Civil War, Washington Arsenal played a pivotal role in provisioning the Union troops with ordnance and ammunition. The acres also presented opportunities for inventors to show off their latest weapons of war. Pres. Abraham Lincoln, a frequent visitor to observe the demonstrations of these weapons, was so impressed with the Agar gun that he purchased 10 of them on the spot.

The arsenal was not without disaster, for on June 14, 1864, a pan of gunpowder stars drying in the sun ignited and set off an explosion in one of the buildings where young women were assembling cartridges. That day, 21 of them lost their lives. When the funeral was held a few days later, Pres. Abraham Lincoln led the procession to Congressional Cemetery, where they were laid to rest.

This late-1800s map shows the artist's interpretation of the capital city at that time and suggests that the Washington Monument had been completed. On Greenleaf Point, the buildings of the Washington Arsenal are distinct. The arsenal, having delivered on the need to provision the Union during the Civil War, lay idle. Some in Congress were calling for its sale, suggesting that the remaining operations move to Fort Myer, which one member of Congress called to rename Fort Grant. (LOC.)

With the river access surrounding the peninsula, this photograph shows some of the inventory of artillery and limbers that were maintained in the Washington Arsenal. Ships would arrive from the north bearing cargo of ordnance produced in the arsenal at Springfield, Massachusetts, along with other foundries. A spur of the railroad went through the arsenal, allowing those items to be shipped where needed during the Civil War. (LOC.)

This early illustration depicts the road leading up to the front of the main building of the Washington Arsenal. Meanwhile, the map at right indicates the buildings (including the magazine, filling workshops, barracks, and guardhouse) that were outside of the arsenal's main building. A railroad line entered from the north and with three spurs provided access to the arsenal, the wharf, and the nearby navy yard. (Above, *Harper's Weekly*; right, NARA.)

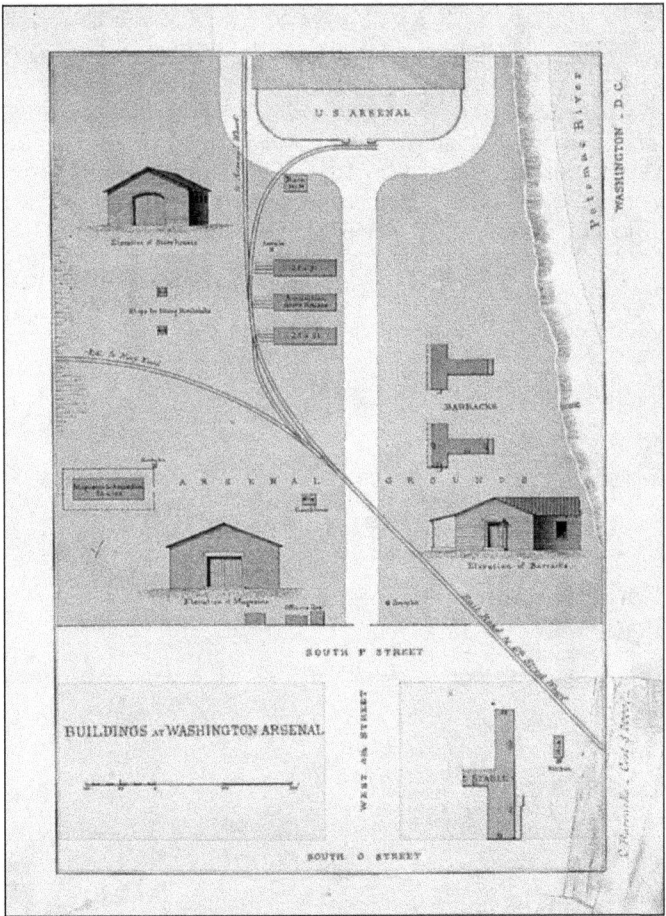

The main arsenal buildings were in the shape of an open quadrangle, providing a "front yard" for the military to enjoy some peaceful time after tending to the day's needs and work. They were separate from the actual workshops and magazines. The photograph below shows where the officers' quarters were inside the quadrangle. (Both, KBH.)

Designed and produced by Wilson Agar, the first rapid-fire machine gun was demonstrated at Washington Arsenal for President Lincoln, who gave it the nickname of "Coffee Mill Gun" since its hopper resembled a coffee mill of the era. The gun had a single barrel, and rounds were fed into the hopper. The rounds were originally metal tubes that contained standard paper cartridges. A separate percussion cap was fitted at the end of the tube. The weapon was fired using a hand crank. Upon seeing this gun in action, Lincoln was very impressed and immediately bought ten. An additional 50 of the guns were later purchased. However, these were hardly used, since the Ordnance Department complained that they consumed too much ammunition. (Both, National Park Service.)

Cannon tubes that arrived from the foundries were placed in inventory storage. The spoke-wheeled gun carriages for the tubes were being built in the shops surrounding the field of tubes. The lower photograph shows how the heavy tubes were dealt with without motorized assistance—heavy cannon tubes were moved and transported by the combination of limber and a sling wagon. In the far background of the image above, one can also see the stacks of cannon balls that were also part of the inventory. (Both, LOC.)

Arsenal workers admire the results of the stacking exercise—ideal and very neat mounds of cannon balls received from the foundry are ready to accompany the next shipment of artillery once their gun carriages were made in the workshop. Thousands of cannonballs produced during the Civil War passed through the Washington Arsenal. (NARA.)

Within the Washington Arsenal, an officer stands in admiration of the long row of artillery available for immediate distribution. The gun tubes would be delivered to the arsenal from the foundries by ship or train, and their gun carriages would be assembled in the workshops to accommodate the various models. The model arsenal building contained scale models of all the different types of ordnance. (NARA.)

The six-pound Wiard rifle was one of two artillery pieces designed by Ontario, Canada–born Norman Wiard. About 60 were manufactured between 1861 and 1862 at O'Donnell's Foundry in New York City. During the Civil War, Wiard served as superintendent of ordnance stores, a post that offered considerable opportunity for his inventive proclivities and, incidentally, brought him into consultation regarding weapons development with both President Lincoln and secretary of war Stanton. (LOC.)

Here is another view of what was stored for distribution at the Washington Arsenal. An artilleryman stands on the trail of the gun carriage, and a row of artillery wagons can be seen the left side of the photograph. In the background, the arsenal building complex can be seen through the stand of trees. (LOC.)

Two artillerymen stand beside their cannons, perhaps in preparation for a demonstration or test of a new batch of artillery assembled here at the Washington Arsenal. Arsenal workers were tasked with a variety of duties. The amount of ordnance shipped thorough the arsenal during the Civil War was staggering. Beyond the testing of artillery, a ballistic pendulum was built to mark the range of the artillery. For images of the pendulum and a map, please consult the accompanying website of www.Historic-FortMcNair.com. (LOC.)

The USS *Bienville* is at the wharf of the Washington Arsenal, where it is loading troops and supplies to head out on a mission. The 1,558-ton-burden wooden side-wheel steamship, built at Brooklyn, New York, in 1860, was purchased by the Navy in August 1861 as part of the great expansion that took place in the first months of the Civil War. (*Harpers Weekly.*)

Arsenal workers look upon a charred wall, all that is left standing after the explosion on June 17, 1864, that claimed the lives of 21 women. The victims were assembling cartridges around a table in the building when sparks from some fireworks stars drying in the sun ignited the gunpowder on the table. (National Defense University Archives.)

The northern front yard of the Washington Arsenal is where the memorial funeral service was held on June 19, 1864, before the procession proceeded to Congressional Cemetery, where the women killed in the explosion would be laid to rest. President Lincoln and secretary of war Edwin Stanton led the procession, which consisted of more than 150 carriages and stretched five miles. (LOC.)

The monument at Congressional Cemetery bears the names of all who perished from the explosion. The workers killed on June 14, 1864, were Melissa Adams, Annie Bache, Emma Baird, Lizzie Brahler, Bettie Branagan, Kate Brosnaham, Mary Burroughs, Emily Collins, Johanna Connors, Bridget Dunn, Susan Harris, Margaret Horan, Rebecca Hull, Eliza Lacey, Louisa Lloyd, Sallie McElfresh, Julia McEwen, Ellen Roche, Pinkey Scott, W.E. Tippett, and Margaret Yonson. (LOC.)

John Quincy Adams was the sixth president of the United States (1825–1829). In 1829, he authorized the building of the first federal penitentiary on the northern end of Greenleaf Point military reservation, then known as Washington Arsenal. Charles Bullfinch, the Boston-born architect of the US Capitol, was chosen to design the penitentiary. (LOC.)

Charles Bullfinch, an American architect, was born in Boston, Massachusetts. He was educated there, notably obtaining both a bachelor's and master's degree at Harvard University. Bullfinch made his name designing Boston buildings; later, he built the Washington Capitol dome and wings. He designed the federal penitentiary placed north of the Washington Arsenal. (Harvard University Portrait Collection.)

Three

A President
Is Assassinated and
a Woman Is Hanged

With the ink barely dry on the surrender papers, it came as a shock that Pres. Abraham Lincoln would be the final casualty of the Civil War. He had a dream that he would be killed, and actor John Wilkes Booth made it a reality when he entered the president's box and with his derringer shot him in the back of the head. The country was in shock. Vice Pres. Andrew Johnson became president and ordered the capture and prosecution of the conspirators who had plotted the death of Lincoln.

Nine people were rounded up, and the ironclad USS *Saugus* was summoned from its patrol of the James River to Washington, DC, to provide the space for the conspirators' initial incarceration. Once it was overloaded, the ironclad USS *Montauk* was also summoned and moored in the river to handle the overflow of prisoners. They were eventually moved to the Federal Penitentiary at Greenleaf Point, with Gen. John Frederick Hartranft as their warden.

The trial was by a military commission of 12 men. They heard the testimony of more than 370 witnesses. It lasted over seven weeks. The hearings were held on the third floor of one of the building extensions from the penitentiary—it is now know as Grant Hall.

War Department, Washington, April 20, 1865,

$100,000 REWARD!

THE MURDERER

Of our late beloved President, Abraham Lincoln,

IS STILL AT LARGE.

$50,000 REWARD

Will be paid by this Department for his apprehension, in addition to any reward offered by Municipal Authorities or State Executives.

$25,000 REWARD

Will be paid for the apprehension of JOHN H SURRATT, one of Booth's Accomplices.

$25,000 REWARD

Will be paid for the apprehension of David C. Harold, another of Booth's accomplices.

EDWIN M. STANTON, Secretary of War.

This wanted poster sadly proclaimed the death of a president. Secretary of war Edwin Stanton was determined to find and bring to justice those who had plotted against the federal government, assassinated Lincoln, and attacked others. Note that the name John Surratt appears on the poster. (LOC.)

The assassin, John Wilkes Booth, had previously plotted among his group to kidnap President Lincoln in return for the release of Confederate prisoners at Point Lookout, Maryland. That plot never was executed. However, Booth, upon hearing Lincoln's Emancipation Proclamation, decided that Lincoln had to be dealt with another way. (LOC.)

This is the derringer that Booth used that fateful April night—it was Good Friday—when Lincoln and his wife were at Ford's Theatre watching a play. Booth used this gun to shoot the president in the back of the head. Lincoln was taken across the street to a boardinghouse now known as the Petersen House, where he died the next morning. (LOC.)

This is Ford's Theater, where Pres. Abraham Lincoln was assassinated. After the assassination, it would be draped in black crepe and have a military guard unit in front of the building. It was here that John Wilkes Booth entered the presidential box and shot the president in the back of the head. He then leaped onto the stage to get away after committing this heinous act. (LOC.)

By military order, President Lincoln's funeral train procession consisted of no fewer than nine cars, including the funeral car, officers' car, six passenger cars, and one baggage car. The procession left Washington, DC, on April 21, 1865, and proceeded across the Northern states, stopping for formal funeral ceremonies in 12 major cities. (LOC.)

Early in April 1865, the US Military Railroad delivered the new presidential railcar, which was produced in Alexandria, Virginia. However, President Lincoln avoided seeing it or riding in it since he did not want to give the impression that money was being wasted after a very costly war. The funeral train was led by a crepe-draped engine bearing the portrait of the slain president on the front. The procession covered 2,000 miles and finally ended up on May 3, 1865, in Springfield, Illinois, where the president's remains were removed to a hearse and brought to his final resting place on May 4. (LOC.)

Lincoln never rode or saw the car while he was alive. After the assassination, the presidential car became the funeral car. It was modified inside to hold the coffins of both president and his son Willie, who had died in 1862 and had been buried in Georgetown. Lincoln's funeral car was destroyed by fire in 1911. (LOC.)

The photograph at left is Mary Surratt's boardinghouse at 604 H Street NW in Washington, DC. It is where the plan to kidnap Abraham Lincoln was plotted. The site is in the National Register of Historic Places and is maintained by the National Park Service. Mary Surratt, pictured below, was the first woman ever convicted and executed by US federal order. She and three other conspirators—George Atzerodt, David E. Herold, and Lewis Payne—were incarcerated, tried, and hanged at the Federal Penitentiary on July 7, 1865, after a seven-week trial by military commission. (Both, LOC.)

This is a very rare image that shows a distant view of the front of the Federal Penitentiary looking south. On the right side is the wharf where the prisoners were transported. In earlier years, the prisoners incarcerated within were tasked with making shoes as a way to support the operation of the facility. (National Defense University Special Collections.)

Once incarcerated within the Federal Penitentiary, the prisoners were kept separated, their heads hooded and their hands manacled. An empty cell was between each of them to ensure that they would not have any communication. A doctor would visit them daily to assure that their health was good. (*Frank Leslie's Illustrated Newspaper.*)

There was a whole fleet of ironclad boats patrolling the coastal waters and rivers of the United States during the Civil War. There were 20 crew members and 9 officers on the *Saugus*. When the number of conspirator prisoners outstripped the space on the Saugus, the USS *Montauk* was summoned to handle the overflow. Eventually, the prisoners were moved to the Federal Penitentiary and Old Capital Prison. (LOC.)

USS *Saugus*, a 2,100-ton Canonicus-class monitor, was built at Wilmington, Delaware. Commissioned in April 1864, it served in the North Atlantic Blockading Squadron during the Civil War's final year, primarily in the James River region. It was summoned to Washington, DC, to hold the prisoners who had conspired to assassinate Lincoln. The bow of the boat could have an extension that was used to sweep for mines. (LOC.)

At some point, it became infeasible for the captured prisoners to be incarcerated on the two ironclad boats—*Saugus* and *Montauk*. A ship was sent to retrieve them for incarceration at the Federal Penitentiary and the Washington Prison. Seen here is the transfer of the manacled prisoners with their hoods, under the dark of night. (*Frank Leslie's Illustrated Newspaper.*)

Born in Raleigh, North Carolina, Andrew Johnson was the 16th vice president of the United States. He assumed office as the 17th president after Abraham Lincoln was assassinated. He gave orders to find and prosecute all the conspirators who had participated in the plot to kill Lincoln. He is the only president to serve in the US Senate after his presidency. (LOC.)

Edwin Stanton was born in Steubenville, Ohio. He was a lawyer who built a successful practice in Ohio, Pittsburgh, then Washington, DC. Lincoln appointed him to his cabinet as secretary of war, where he did a fine job eliminating corruption. When Lincoln was assassinated, Stanton pushed to locate and try the conspirators who had plotted to kill the president. (LOC.)

Known from 1815 to 1819 as the Old Brick Capitol (after the British had burned the Capitol during the War of 1812), this facility later became the Old Capital Prison during the Civil War. After President Lincoln was assassinated, several of the accused conspirators were incarcerated there, including Dr. Samuel Mudd, Mary Surratt, Louis Weichmann, and John T. Ford, owner of Ford's Theatre. (LOC.)

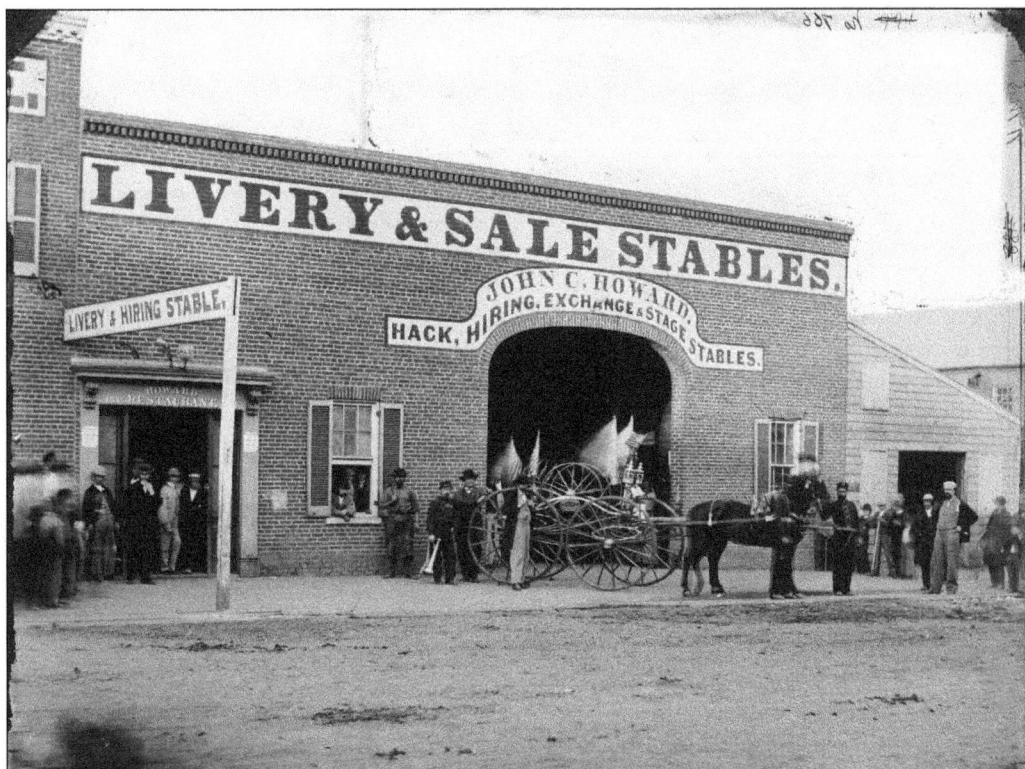

This is the John C. Howard Livery Stables on G Street between Sixth and Seventh Streets in Washington, DC. It was here that John Harrison Surratt kept his horses before leaving town on April 1, 1865. It was also where John Wilkes Booth hired a horse to get away after carrying out the assassination of Pres. Abraham Lincoln on Friday, April 14, 1865. (LOC.)

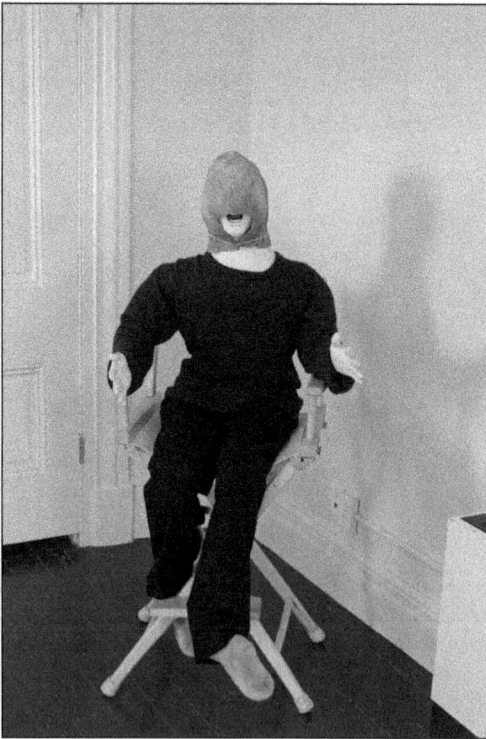

The accused assassination conspirators were very closely controlled while not in the courtroom. They were kept in the dark and secured in cells within the penitentiary. Additionally, they were outfitted with a hood, as seen at left, which only allowed them to breathe and eat or drink. Secured to their ankle was the 50-pound ball and chain. (Photographs by John Michael.)

John Frederick Hartranft was a major general in the Union army during the Civil War. At the end of the war, Hartranft was appointed special provost marshal for the trial of the Lincoln assassination conspirators. As such, he was responsible for the custody of the prisoners and for eventually supervising the execution of four of those convicted. Hartranft was especially noted for his kind treatment toward Mary Surratt, the first woman ever executed by the federal government. (LOC.)

As provost marshal, Maj. Gen. John Hartranft had responsibility for the conspirators. His staff, which included a doctor, was, from left to right, Capt. R.A. Watts, Lt. Col. George W. Frederick, Lt. Col William H.H. McCall, Lt. D.H. Geissinger, General Hartranft, assistant surgeon George L. Porter, Col. L.A. Dodd, and Capt. Christian Rath. (LOC.)

David Hunter was born in Troy, New York. An 1822 graduate of the US Military Academy, he served as a major general during the Civil War. He was known for his General Order No. 11 on April 25, 1862, which freed the slaves in Florida, Georgia, and South Carolina. It was later rescinded. (LOC.)

Maj. Gen. David Hunter commanded the military commission who tried the Lincoln assassination conspirators. Standing from left to right are Brig. Gen. Thomas M. Harris, Maj. Gen. Lew Wallace, Maj. Gen. August V. Kautz, and Henry L. Burnett. Seated from left to right are Lt. Col. David R. Clendenin, Col. C.H. Tompkins, Brig. Gen. Albion P. Howe, Brig. Gen. James Ekin, Maj. Gen. David Hunter, Brig. Gen. Robert S. Foster, John A. Bingham, and Brig. Gen. Joseph Holt. (LOC.)

This illustration is a depiction of the third-floor courtroom where the Lincoln assassination conspirators were tried by a military commission. The trial lasted from April to July 7, 1865, and included the testimony of more than 370 witnesses. Four of the conspirators were convicted and sentenced to be hanged. (*Frank Leslie's Illustrated Newspaper.*)

Building No. 20, also known as Grant Hall, is where the trial took place. In 1865, it was connected to the Federal Penitentiary via the door at rear left. This is the room as it appears today. It went through extensive remodeling after all the changes that occurred during the past decades. (USA.)

After seven weeks of hearings, the military commission announced its verdicts regarding the conspirators. Four were to hang on July 7, 1865. The gallows were built very near where the trial was held, and the noise of construction could be heard during the proceedings. On Friday, the prisoners—Mary Surratt, George Atzerodt, David E. Herold, and Lewis Payne—were brought from their cells, made to climb the stairs, and then read their sentences. (Both, LOC.)

After they were read their sentences, ropes were placed around their necks, their legs were bound together, and hoods were placed over their heads. Next, the supports were removed under the platform, allowing them to drop and hang. After they had all expired, their bodies were removed and placed in shallow graves near the gallows. It was not long before the penitentiary was abandoned and torn down, the bricks reused to build the wall around the post. The executions were a event that was begging to be forgotten. (*Frank Leslie's Illustrated Newspaper.*)

Lew Wallace was a general in the Civil War. He was born in Brookville, Indiana. Although he did not attend any military school, he began a militia in Indiana that was his launch into the military with some success. Known for his writing, he is the author of the book *Ben-Hur*. He also served as a member of the military commission that tried the Lincoln assassination conspirators. (LOC.)

Based on the trial and the findings of the military commission, four convicted conspirators were hanged on July 7, 1865, at the gallows within the Federal Penitentiary on Greenleaf Point in Washington, DC. This is a section of rope that was used to carry out the executions. (LOC.)

Maj. Gen. Winfield Scott Hancock was a Union general whose four decades of service included the Mexican-American War and the Civil War. He was an 1844 graduate of the US Military Academy. He was assigned to supervise the execution of the Lincoln assassination conspirators, and he carried out his orders, later writing that "every soldier was bound to act as I did under similar circumstances." (LOC.)

John Harrison Surratt was one of the Lincoln conspirators who got away. He was involved in the plot to kidnap Lincoln, but had no involvement in the assassination. When Lincoln was shot by John Wilkes Booth, John Surratt fled first to Canada, then to Europe, where he joined the Papal Zouaves under an alias. Later arrested and tried for his involvement, he was set free because of a mistrial. (LOC.)

After the US Civil War, the acres were renamed to Washington Barracks. Upon entering the front gate of the post, which is decorated with the tubes of cannons from the foundry in Richmond, Virginia, this guardhouse was the first building that was encountered. Inside of this building is where the soldiers guarding the entrance were stationed. (KBH.)

There were two hospitals on the installation. This was considered the post hospital, where the soldiers, who were garrisoned at the installation, were treated. The medical staff there tended to the needs and illnesses of the soldiers and their families. (KBH.)

Maj. Walter Reed was born in Gloucester County, Virginia. After securing two medical degrees, Reed joined the US Army Medical Corps. His last tour of duty was with the 7th Artillery at Washington Barracks. It was while there that he discovered that yellow fever was transmitted by a mosquito. His findings allowed the resumption of the completion of the Panama Canal. In November 1902, Reed's appendix ruptured; he died on November 22, 1902, of the resulting peritonitis, at age 51. (NARA.)

Soldiers garrisoned here had a good selection of medical services given the size of the post and the number of troops garrisoned. This is another of the medical facilities on post: the dental clinic and dispensary that provided medical treatment for ailing soldiers and their family members. (KBH.)

This is US Army Medical Hospital within Washington Barracks. Maj. Walter Reed practiced medicine in this building up until his bout with appendicitis. When he was operated on for the condition, he died. Later reports have suggested that he haunts the site. (KBH.)

The legacy of the doctor lives on in that Walter Reed Army Hospital, a tribute to Maj. Walter Reed, opened on May 1, 1909, just seven years after his death. The hospital on Washington Barracks closed, and all staff and treatment moved to the new facility within Washington, DC. The hospital developed a reputation for delivering top-notch medical treatment. (LOC.)

Four

THE ENGINEERS ARRIVE, AND A MOST BEAUTIFUL US ARMY POST IS BUILT

The US Army Engineering School claimed the acres of Greenleaf Point, then known as Washington Barracks, from 1901 to 1919. A significant construction project took place when 57 buildings were erected in the early years: barracks, officers' and NCO housing, stables, the hospital, the officers' club, and more. Overall, construction was a challenge, particularly given the swampy acreage of Greenleaf Point and the two rivers.

Most notable among the buildings was the McKim, Mead & White–designed Beaux Arts–style edifice that became the Army War College, also known as Roosevelt Hall. The cornerstone was laid on February 21, 1903, in a ceremony by Pres. Theodore Roosevelt. Construction was finished in 1907, and the first graduating class of the college finished in 1909. Among the early decorative items was a statue of Frederick the Great that stood firmly in front of where Roosevelt Hall was constructed. The statue was intended to be joined by other statues of several additional military greats.

Meanwhile, with construction completed on post, the engineers continued to train their soldiers in a variety of skills, such as photography, masonry, bridge building, electrical motors, and mechanical processes.

In 1918, the movie *His Greatest Gift* was filmed on post, with trenches dug to simulate the World War I battlefield. Soldiers on post were the actors of the day. The weather cooperated, and ground was snow covered, which provided the film crew great opportunity to capture the movie.

Theodore "Teddy" Roosevelt was the 26th president of the United States and is known for his accomplishments as a Rough Rider in the Spanish-American War and his great love of the outdoors and hunting (the teddy bear is named after him because of his hunting trip in Mississippi and a political cartoon published in the *Washington Post* newspaper lampooning his action by Clifford Kennedy Berryman). With Elihu Root as secretary of war, he laid a foundation to transform the military to respond to events and preserve the peace. (LOC.)

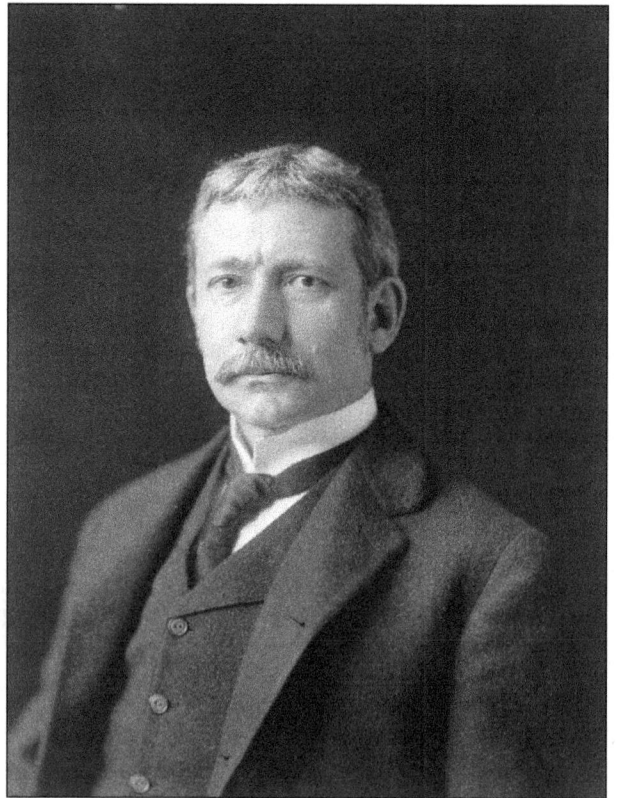

Elihu Root was born in Clinton, New York. A lawyer, he was secretary of war under two US presidents. It was under Theodore Roosevelt that he proposed and implemented sweeping plans to transform the US military. One of the initial outcomes was the Army War College and the building of Roosevelt Hall at Washington Barracks. (LOC.)

THE PRESIDENT DELIVERING HIS ADDRESS.

Roosevelt Hall began the new transition of the US military—its cornerstone was laid on February 21, 1903, by Pres. Theodore Roosevelt, and on June 30, 1907, the building was occupied for the first time. (KBH.)

The cornerstone sits waiting for the rest of the new Army War College to surround it. In the background are the remaining buildings of the Washington Arsenal; they were later razed and the land cleared. Rubble from the old arsenal buildings was used to bolster the seawall around Greenleaf Point. (KBH.)

The statue of Frederick the Great, donated by Emperor Wilhelm II, was the first military leader to grace the front of the Army War College building, Roosevelt Hall. There were plans to have statues of other military greats placed adjacent; those would include Caesar, Hannibal, Alexander, Suvaroff, and Wellington. (KBH.)

The plans for the building were very well engineered. The massive structure would rise to nearly 130 feet at its highest elevation. The foundation had to be sturdy, and support of the building was complemented with reinforced construction. (KBH.)

Roosevelt Hall was not the only building under construction in the early 1900s. A row of 15 officers' quarters, the officers' club, barracks, and more were also being added to the post's inventory of new buildings. This necessitated an on-site cement mixer to provide the workers adequate materials to complete construction. (KBH)

Intricate scaffolding provides easy access to for workers completing Roosevelt Hall. This view is of the front of the building, with the roof already in place. Finishing touches to the decorative aspect of the building are next. (KBH.)

In this photograph from an earlier phase of construction, the statue of Frederick the Great is isolated, with fencing for protection from harm during the work. The outhouse to its left is not there for Freddy. (KBH.)

War College, looking N.W., Oct. 28. 1905.

As the building rose in height, additional intricate scaffolding was added to allow the workmen to finish the building. Cranes and gantries on the top allowed for easy delivery of materials. (KBH.)

Here, workers are razing and building at the same time—the south side of Roosevelt Hall on the left shows a variety of old Washington Arsenal buildings that are still intact. Those will be coming down, their materials salvaged or used for the seawall. A clear vista to the Potomac River is the plan. (KBH.)

This view from the southwest shows Roosevelt Hall after the old arsenal buildings have been removed. The scaffolding on the left of the photograph surrounds the place where internally will be the lecture hall auditorium. (KBH.)

It is June 1907. After over four years of construction, Roosevelt Hall is ready to accommodate the students of the Army War College. The statue of Frederick the Great stands proudly in front of the new building. Several other statues were considered when this one showed up. However, no one else decided to make a donation of any additional statues. (KBH.)

A view from the southern end of the peninsula shows the back of Roosevelt Hall with a clear line of sight. All the old arsenal buildings have been cleared. The rounded center of the building is where the lecture auditorium is placed. (KBH.)

Here is a view from the west showing the fine styling of the building and the intricate, repeating design that is also on the north side of Roosevelt Hall—the new Army War College. (LOC.)

The beauty continues on the inside of the building. Here is the top of one of the support columns. Not only is it functional, holding up the building and roof, but it also features an intricate and long-lasting design. (LOC.)

With a unique shelving system in place from Snead and Company, the library within the Army War College was easily accessible. The college received an extensive collection that had until that time been housed at the War Department. Tens of thousands of items were transferred to provide reference material for the students. It was the Snead system (also used by the Library of Congress) that allowed the volume of items to be stored in a compact space. The ceiling of the building is graced with a layer of tiles (Both, LOC.)

Here is the first graduating class (1909–1910) from the new Army War College. Of the more than 30 graduates, many would go on to reach the rank of general officer. One, in fact, was Lt. Col. John A. Lejeune, who rose through the ranks in the US Marine Corps to become commandant. For the identities of those persons in the image, please refer to the accompanying complementary website www.Historic-FortMcnair.com. (NARA.)

Outstanding graduates are the outcome of an outstanding faculty. These 20 men provided the direction and instruction that helped to develop the skills and experience in the members of the graduating class. For the identities of those persons in the image, please refer to the accompanying complementary website www.Historic-FortMcnair.com. (NARA.)

Since the land Fort McNair is built upon was mostly a marshy swamp, it was necessary to take extra precautions when the row of officers' housing and the officers' club were being constructed. Concrete pilings were formed (above) and sunk among the footings of the foundations of the buildings. (Both, KBH.)

Here is a view from the southwest corner of the new officers' club under construction. The building of it coincided with the construction of the Army War College building and many more edifices on post. The post was a continual work in progress from 1903 to 1907 with all the new construction. (KBH.)

Here are the nearly completed officers' quarters. It was no small feat that 15 of these quarters were constructed simultaneously. Here, the roofs are awaiting the slate shingles, which will be applied next (KBH.)

Months later, and the officers' club and the officers' quarters are complete on the outside and are awaiting landscaping and the roadwork to be done. All of them show a fine example of Colonial style with their bright white columns. (KBH.)

Landscaping completed, here is a frontal view of one of the 15 officers' quarters. The front of the house faces the parade field, while the back of the dwelling has a great water view of the Potomac River. (KBH.)

The photograph shows the tree-lined street of all the quarters with a complement roadway on the river side of the row. This layout plan provides on-street parking for the residents. The photograph below shows the officers' club view from the Potomac River. (Both, KBH.)

Housing for the noncommissioned officers was also being constructed at the same time across the parade field. The cement mixer must have been running all day and night to keep up with the demand for concrete. (KBH.)

By March 1905, the mess hall and kitchen to feed the troops was nearly completed. It would be a great service to the soldiers to provide a central place to go to for their meals. (KBH.)

Housing for the enlisted men was also under construction during that building period of 1901–1907. Here are Barracks No. 2 (above) and No. 1 (below). The larger one would one day house the Alpha Company of the 3rd Infantry—"the Old Guard." The company would also become "the Commander-in-Chief's Guard" in 1974. Below, the smaller barracks would eventually be the home of the US Army Music School and later house the Inter-American Defense College. (Both, KBH.)

During the 1900s, the US Army still moved by horse (and mule), so there was a need for some fine stables to accommodate the mounts of the soldiers. In a few years, the US Army would establish the remount service with a remount depot in Front Royal, Virginia. Fresh horses would be available to fill both of these stables. (Both, KBH.)

Pictured above are the model arsenal building (right) and what was originally the guardhouse. The photograph below shows the guardhouse building, which was constructed in 1882 using the bricks from the old penitentiary. Later, the building would be gutted to become the photograph lab for the engineering school. After another remodeling, it would serve as quarters. (Both, KBH.)

These are NCO quarters from the Washington Arsenal time frame. When the building boom began in 1901, they were razed and replaced by the new NCO quarters shown on page 68. Wood-frame quarters were replaced by brick and mortar. (KBH.)

ADMINISTRATION BUILDING.

What once had been the model arsenal built in 1838, where displays of 1:4–sized models of ordnance were kept, now became the administration building for the engineering school. Once the engineers left in 1919, it would once again go through a remodeling and become quarters for married soldiers. (KBH.)

With the Federal Penitentiary gone, building No. 20 took on a new life. Once the location of the trial of the Lincoln assassination conspirators, it now was remodeled to accommodate the need for more housing on post. (KBH.)

Inter- and intraservice football was a mainstay activity in the military. Football had been introduced at West Point in 1890. Meanwhile, teams were formed on military installations to compete both among the military and collegiate teams. This is the team the engineers fielded, which included both enlisted men and officers. (KBH.)

The US Army Engineering School was located at Willets Point, New York, when it was ordered to move to Washington Barracks. Announcing the arrival and looking for new recruits, these two posters (in color) announced what the engineering course within the US Army would provide in terms of skills and new experiences. These posters are in full color and can be seen with other associated recruiting posters on the accompanying complementary website www.Historic-FortMcnair.com. (Both, LOC.)

Engineers Auto Repair School offered great challenges to the soldier. Here, enlisted men are given a one-month course in practical and elementary theoretical auto repair. In this course, automobiles and trucks are taken apart and completely reassembled from the ground up by the student engineer enlisted man. (NARA.)

Another engineering school was focused on electricity. In this school, the student engineer learned about electricity and the handling of electrical machinery. The basics of power and the complete overhaul of machinery were also covered. (NARA.)

Despite the end of the arsenal, there was still demand for the production of limbers and caissons. One engineering school continued the tradition of assembling and repairing limbers and caissons for the field. Many branches of the US Army used these horse-drawn vehicles to get where they needed. (NARA.)

Students from the Army War College are on a field trip. They are encountering real-time issues in the field in order to gain practical experience that will give them the foundation to make decisions in the future, whether it be in a combat role or in the day-to-day needs of their assignment. (NARA.)

The US Army Signal Corps came to visit Washington Barracks and brought some of their equipment with them. Searchlights were mounted on a caisson and towed by a limber. Searchlights were used in combat up until World War II and provided a way to spot the invading enemy, whether on the ground or in the air. (Both, NARA.)

These two photographs prove the effectiveness of using searchlights to light up the night. The above photograph shows how the lights illuminate the grounds around them, almost turning things into daylight. The second photograph provides a similar result when the light is cast on another area of the post at night. (Both, NARA.)

In 1918, after the end of World War I, a movie was filmed on post titled *His Greatest Gift*. It included soldiers from the post, and the weather cooperated by providing a good blanket of snow. The intent was to represent a battleground of World War I. In the image above, an officer is providing background about the action. Below, in the background, a couple of officers' quarters are visible as the soldiers go through their actions. (Both, NARA.)

Trenches were dug, and doughboy uniforms—including helmets—were used to simulate a World War I battlefield in the above photograph. Below, meanwhile, the officers meet to review the day's work. One can see their tents to the left and Barracks No. 2 in the background. (Both, NARA.)

Five

The Army Teaches Defense, Music, Entertainment, and New Artillery

The US Army Music School was on post when the name Washington Barracks was again assigned to the post. The Army Engineering School, even after it built its own building, went across the river to what is now Fort Belvoir, Virginia. Meanwhile, the music school occupied the barracks next to the hospital. The US Army Band, as requested by Gen. John "Blackjack" Pershing, was organized and constituted at Fort Hunt, Virginia, near Mount Vernon. In 1922, the US Army abandoned Fort Hunt and then sent Pershing's Own across the river to Washington Barracks. There it stayed and played until 1942, then it moved to Fort Myer, Virginia. Later, the band was deployed to the Atlantic theater in World War II. Upon the end of its deployment, the band returned to Fort Myer, Virginia.

The music school trained many musicians for the numerous bands that the US Army had in those days. Among them were "mounted musicians," since many of the bands were mounted on horseback, such as those for the field artillery and cavalry.

Maj. Gen. James William McAndrew, commandant of the Army War College, addresses the class of 1920 while Gen. John "Blackjack" Pershing looks on. The class size continues to grow. This class graduated 75 between officers from the US Army and the US Marine Corps. One among them will become the commandant of the Army War College. It would be Maj. Gen. Hanson Edward Ely (Both, NARA.)

Gen. John "Blackjack" Pershing (left) and Maj. Gen. Hanson Edward Ely (right) stand on the Army War College steps in the photograph at right. General Ely was born in Independence, Iowa, and was a 1891 graduate of the US Military Academy. After a variety of assignments, he was named commandant of the Army War College. In the photograph below, he stands with his staff on the same steps of Roosevelt Hall. (Both, NARA.)

The US Army Band had its beginnings in 1922 at Fort Hunt, Virginia. When the Army abandoned Fort Hunt, the band moved to what then was Washington Barracks. It was in good company, since the US Army Music School was also on post and had taken over Barracks No. 1. The band found its practice room in the gymnasium on post, though better accommodations were forthcoming. The photograph below shows the band in support of a funeral at Arlington National Cemetery. (Both, NARA.)

Now settled in its new quarters in Washington, DC, the band continued to provide support for major events. It was following General Pershing's order. In the above photograph, the band poses wearing its new uniforms on the steps of the Army War College. Below, it shows off the new uniforms as it marches in the Defense Day parade in downtown Washington, DC. (Both, NARA.)

In July 1938, the US Army Band, known also as "Pershing's Own," traveled to Gettysburg, Pennsylvania, to participate in the 75th anniversary of the Battle of Gettysburg. Soon, it would be heading "over there" to entertain the troops during World War II. Before its deployment to North Africa, it would bid Washington Barracks farewell and end up at Fort Myer, Virginia. (Both, NARA.)

When the US Army Engineering School left Washington Barracks and went to Fort Belvoir, Virginia, the US Army Music School then occupied barracks No. 1. Here are the students of the school getting a chalkboard lesson in music. Soldiers from all over the country would come to learn to play in a band. (NARA.)

Here is a graduating class of flute players holding onto their instruments while posing in front of barracks No. 1, where the US Army Music School was located. Instruction included a variety of instruments to fill the needs of the various bands across the country within the Army. (NARA.)

When instruments broke, the US Army Music School repaired them on site. Here is the instrument-repair room in Barracks No. 1, with two soldiers hard at work fixing some broken instruments. (NARA.)

Also seen in front of the US Army Music School headquarters, an entire band of regimental or division size poses with instruments. In addition to marching bands, soldiers were trained for service with bands mounted on horseback. That need would not last long, for as World War II broke out, the US Army mechanized and began abandoning the horse. (NARA.)

Soldiers were expected to keep things neat and squared away. In these photographs, the locker, foot trunk, and bed are all ready for an inspection. When there was not much going on, inspections like this would occur frequently to keep the soldiers out of trouble. (Both, NARA.)

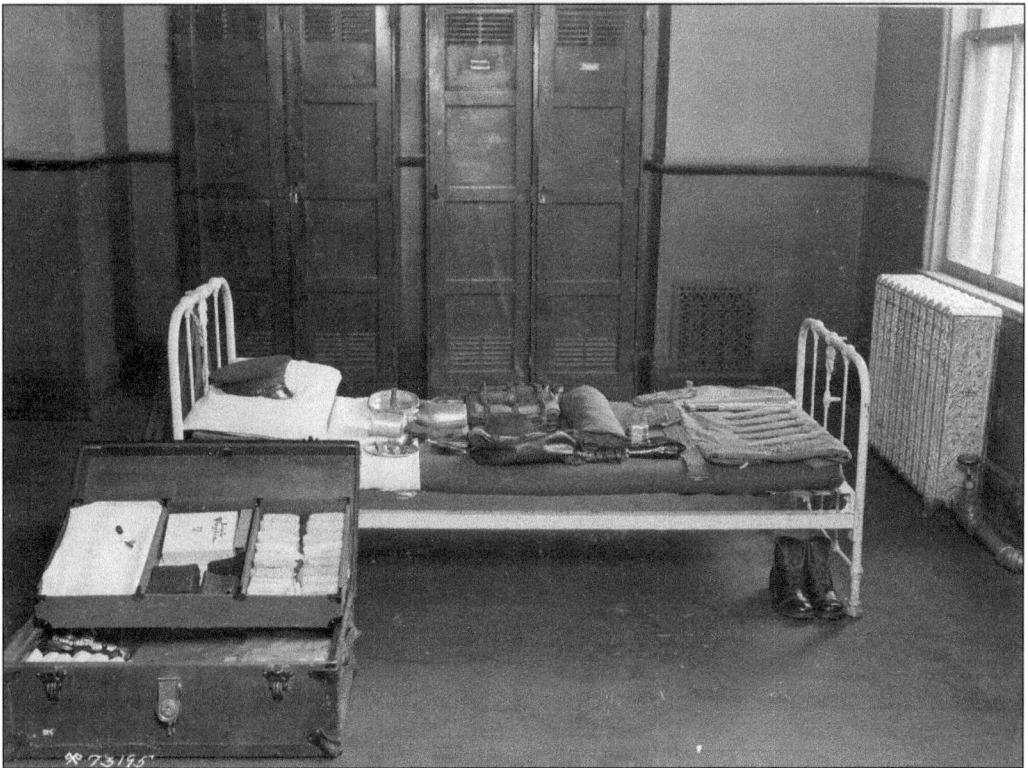

This aerial photograph was taken sometime in the early 1920s, for the golf course is nowhere to be seen. The nine-hole course would be installed in 1929 and provide entertainment for the residents until 2003. (NARA.)

This is a water view from the Potomac River. The wharf from the Washington Arsenal days is gone, burned and not replaced. In later years, a marina would be established on the east side of the peninsula, providing water access for the boating types. (LOC.)

In 1933, George H. Dern was secretary of war. He is pictured here, second from left, at the Army War College at Washington Barracks for a radio broadcast. Standing with him are, at left, Maj. Gen. George Simonds, commandant of the Army War College, Capt. Kendall Fielder, commanding officer of the Army Band (second from right), and Capt. William Stannard, leader of the Army Band (right). (NARA.)

Gen. Charles Pelot Summerall was named chief of staff of the Army. In his honor, a reception was given at the Washington Barracks officers' club. He is seen here arriving at the club on post in his chauffeured car. (NARA.)

Between wars, when there was not much to do, a carnival was held at Washington Barracks. These two images show some of the booths and attractions that were presented during the event. Funds raised from the event were donated to the Army Relief Fund, which benefited soldiers in need. (Both, NARA.)

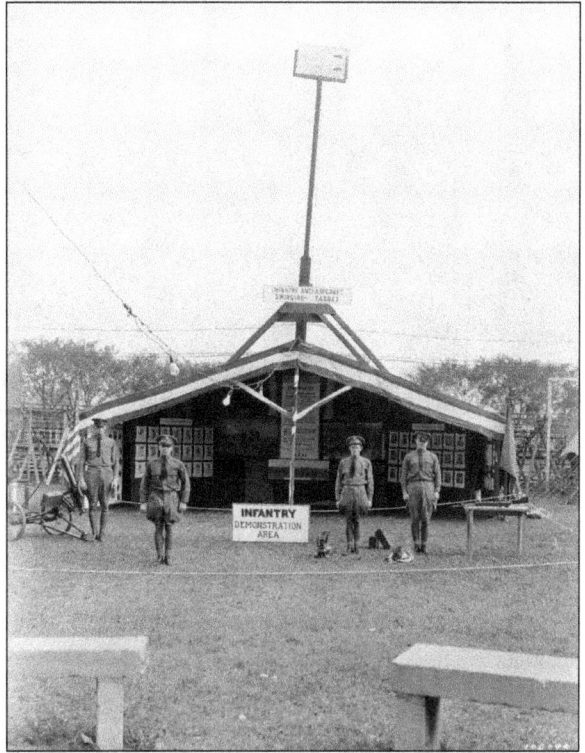

At the same carnival, various displays of US Army branches and specialties were presented to also allow recruiting at the event. Here is a display from the Infantry with an exhibit of its rifles. Other branches, such as the Signal Corps, Corps of Engineers, Armor, and more would also have booths. (Both, NARA.)

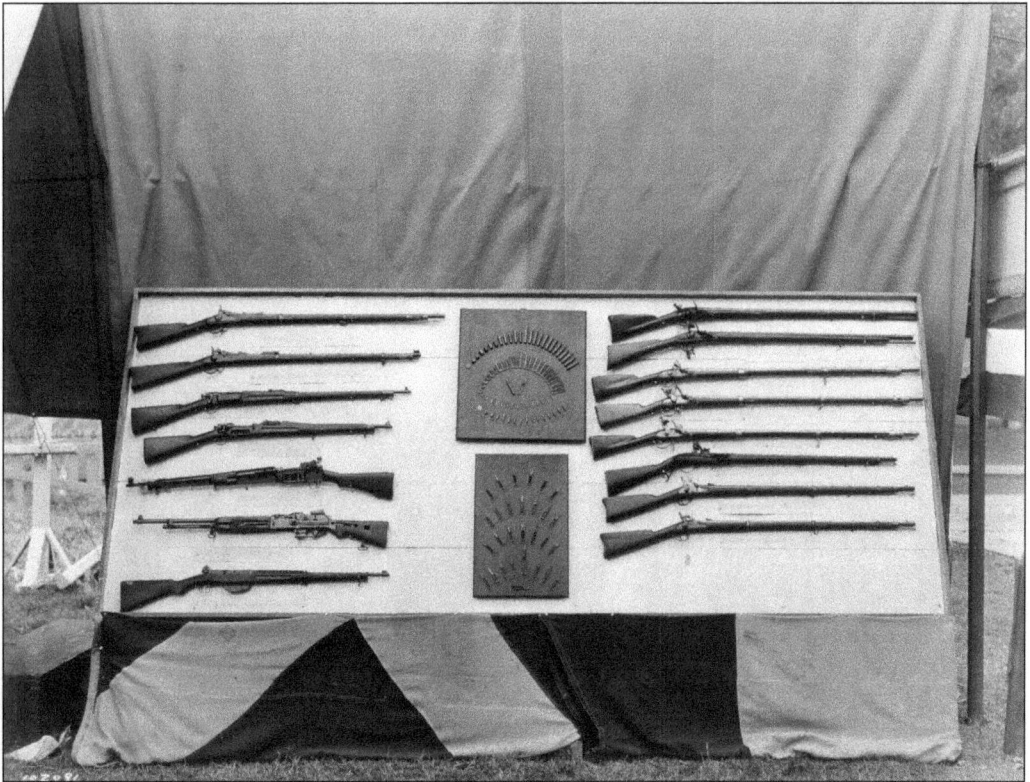

The 17th Field Artillery from Fort Bragg, North Carolina, came to visit. At left, it is passing by the flagpole on the parade field. Note the white megaphone in use before there were public address systems. The flagpole also is surrounded by an array of captured artillery. The photograph below shows the unit in its trucks, with artillery pieces in tow, parked in front of the Army War College at Roosevelt Hall. (Both, NARA.)

The 17th Field Artillery came to show off its new artillery. In the photograph above are, from left to right, Maj. Gen. Harry G. Bienop, chief of field artillery; Maj. Gen. George Van Horn Moseley, deputy chief of staff; and Gen. Peyton Marsh, retired former chief of staff. The gun is a 75-millimeter Model 1897 mounted on an M123 carriage. Below, the 17th Field Artillery poses with its new gun. (Both, NARA.)

Maj. Gen. Andrew Atkinson Humphreys was born in Philadelphia, Pennsylvania. A 1831 graduate of the US Military Academy, he was a career Army officer. He was named chief engineer of the US Army. Washington Barracks was briefly named Fort Humphreys in his honor, but it reverted back to being called Army War College. Fort Belvoir, Virginia, was also briefly called Fort Humphreys. (NARA.)

This photograph, which was taken from a building's rooftop, looks south with Roosevelt Hall in the far background. The parade field can be seen in the foreground on the left. Among the other buildings close by is the US Army hospital where Maj. Walter Reed practiced. (NARA.)

Six

A General Is Killed in Action and a Fort Is His Tribute

When a general or a flag officer (Navy) is killed, especially in action, it is a rare occurrence. But in the throes of war, no one can really predict what will happen, or to whom. Lt. Gen. Lesley J. McNair was truly not in harm's way when an error caused a bomb to fall into his foxhole. The results were disastrous. In recognition, he got an Army post named after him, for he commanded all the Army ground forces in World War II.

One of the most prestigious units was brought to Fort McNair to provide for a defensive capability. The 3rd Infantry Regiment's Alpha Company was the first company formed when the regiment was reactivated on April 6, 1948. Part of those plans to defend the capital included moving Alpha Company of the 3rd Infantry Regiment, "the Old Guard," to Fort McNair. When the 3rd had been reactivated after the war, the ceremonial company of the US Army Military District of Washington (MDW) became Alpha, continuing on the role of the premier ceremonial unit of the US Army. In 1974, in anticipation of the US bicentennial, Alpha Company also took on the role of the "Commander-in-Chief's Guard." Its third uniform was the Colonial dress of blue coats and tricorne hats, along with the white wigs and issued Brown Bess muskets.

In this aerial photograph, Potomac Park is shown with its golf course, and Hains Point (honoring the work of Maj. Gen. Peter Conover Hains, who designed the Tidal Basin to solve the drainage problems) is at the southern tip. Judging by the view of Greenleaf Point and the post, it is still prior to 1929, as there is no golf course. (NARA.)

Looking to the northwest, with Roosevelt Hall in mid-ground, the sand traps of the golf course are clearly visible. A round would include nine holes. The golf course, which disappeared in the autumn of 2003, is now only a distant memory. (LOC.)

The quartermaster stables were remodeled and turned into the post's movie theater. With spacious seating, it could allow the troops from the entire post to watch a movie. Prices then were very reasonable also. (Both, KBH.)

In the above photograph, Gen. Lesley J. McNair (right) meets with an umpire to get feedback on the training exercise that just occurred. General McNair trained his troops at then Washington Barracks. Below, General McNair stands in front of a portrait painted by Sergeant Cummings, whose wife stands next to him. (Above, LOC; below, KBH.)

Gen. Lesley J. McNair was killed in World War II at Normandy. He is buried at the Normandy Cemetery. When he died, his rank was lieutenant general; he was promoted to full general after his death. These two photographs document the promotion. The lower photograph has the designation "LT GEN" for lieutenant general, which was his rank prior to his death. The photograph at right has the designation "GEN" for general. The American Battle Monuments Commission was only alerted in 2010 of his promotion, and a new stone was placed. (Right, Carol Pollard; below, Angela Ponte.)

When the Potomac River rises above its banks because of heavy rains or increased snowmelt, Fort McNair suffers the consequences. There was flooding in 1936, and again in 1942, when the river overflowed its banks, and the results were damaging. Above, no land can be seen as the river's waters have surrounded the temporary building in the background. At left, the east wall is seen as the rising waters cover all the land. (Both, NARA.)

Two soldiers are pictured in a small boat with filled sandbags to their left. The caption penciled in on this photograph, taken during the flood of 1936, read "Rio d' War College." In the photograph below, two other soldiers walk toward the receding waters to inspect the damage done by the flood. (Both, NARA.)

The US Army Signal Corps film-processing plant, also located on post, produced training films for the Army War College. This building was the storehouse for those films. Situated at the northwest side of Roosevelt Hall, it contained vaults where the films were stored. (Both, LOC.)

The vault either contained canisters or cabinets with drawers to hold the processed film. The films were stored there until the 1970s, when they were transferred to the National Archives facility in Suitland, Maryland. In the late 1970s, a fire broke out one day when the films spontaneously combusted. It is believed that the World War I film *His Greatest Gift*, which was captured on the acres then known as the Army War College, was lost in that fire (See pages 79–80). (Both, NARA.)

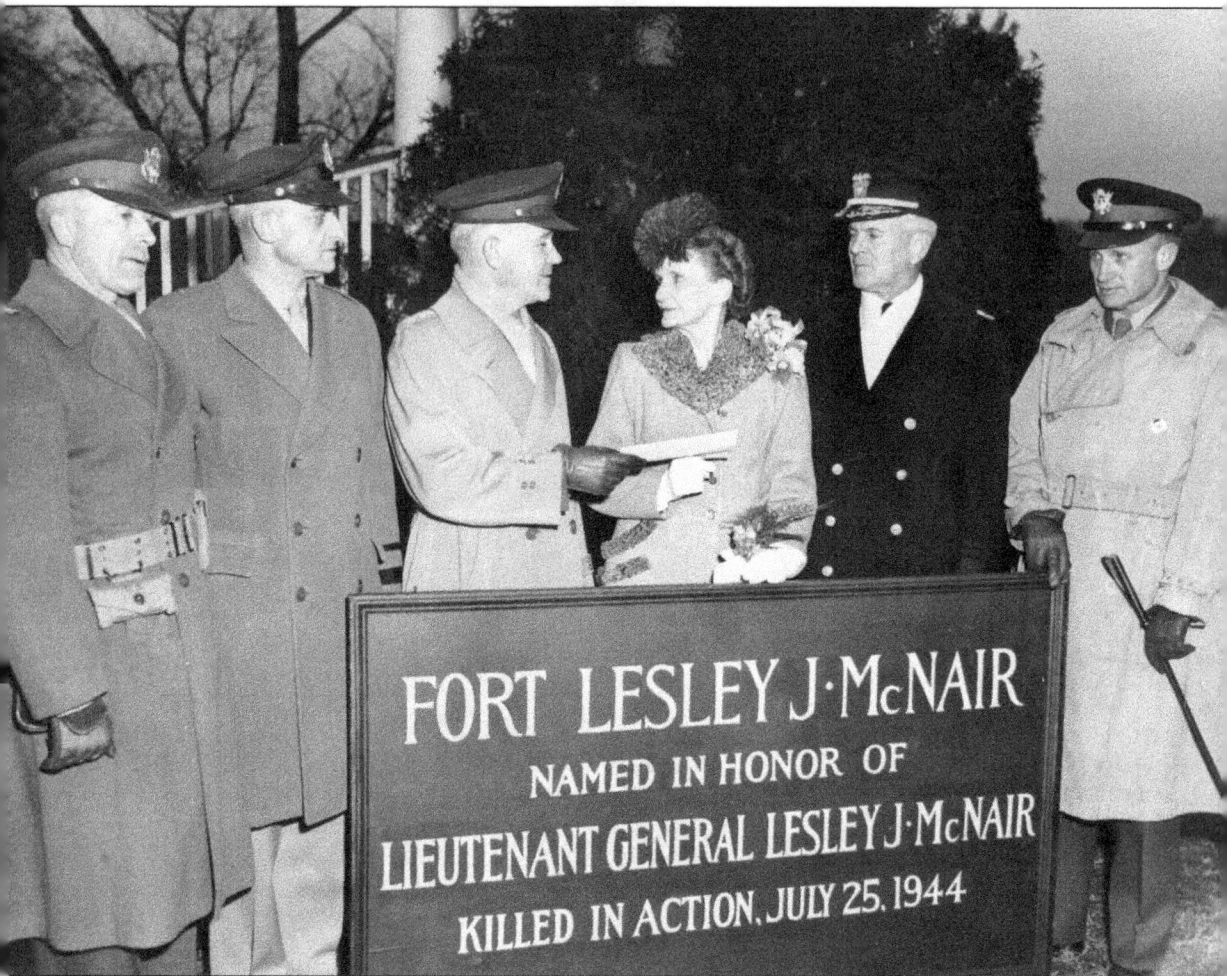

In 1948, Washington Barracks was no more. The post now bears the name of General McNair, who was killed in World War II. He was the highest-ranking US Army officer to die in World War II. Here, from left to right, Col. Charles H. Owens, post commander, is pictured along with Generals McKinley and Collins; McNair's wife, Clare; Vice Admiral Hill; and Brigadier General Gray at the dedication in 1948. (KBH.)

When the 3rd Infantry Regiment of the US Army was reactivated on April 6, 1948, the Military District of Washington's Ceremonial Company was rolled into the new Alpha Company of the Old Guard. Alpha has been the first company of the regiment. It was moved to Fort McNair to assure response if an emergency arose within Washington, DC. In 1974, the company was given another honor: the privilege of being the "Commander-in-Chief's Guard." It wears the Colonial uniform as described by Washington. (Both, USA.)

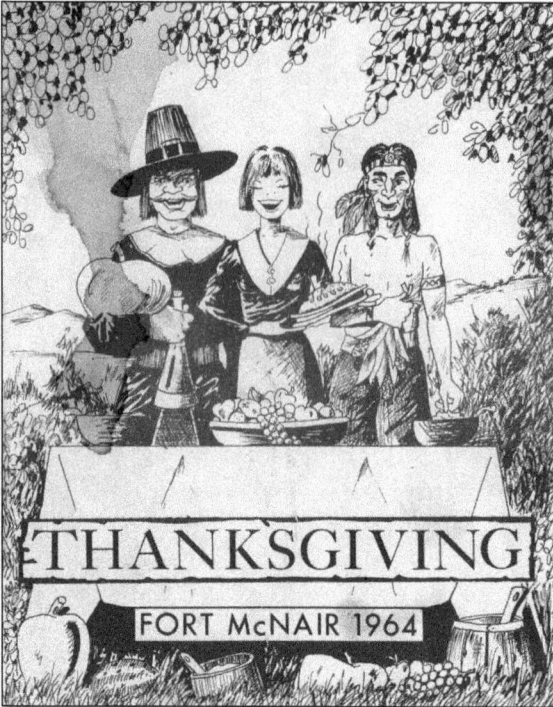

This is the cover of the 1964 Thanksgiving menu at Fort Lesley J. McNair. At that time, the post's commander was Col. Horace E. Townsend. Included in the menu were Thanksgiving greetings from both the commander and the Military District of Washington's acting commander, Col. Louis Gershenow. The entire menu and the letters are available at www.Historic-FortMcNair.com. (US Army–Old Guard Museum.)

This is Alpha Company of the 3rd Infantry US Army. When they are acting as the "Commander-in-Chief's Guard," they carry "Brown Bess" muskets with long bayonets. They fire cartridges that need to be tamped with a tamping rod. When they march, their movements are reflective of the way that marching was done during Colonial times. Their combat tactics also reflect those times. (USA.)

Seven

A Short Tour
Around the Most
Beautiful Army Post

Today, Fort Lesley J. McNair has found its final niche. There are no more name changes and no more significant construction. The National Defense University and several of its colleges are providing the main ongoing activity. From time to time, events such as retirements, graduation ceremonies, or perhaps the Twilight Tattoo are held on the spacious field in front of Roosevelt Hall. The Twilight Tattoo is held weekly during the summer months by the Military District of Washington and showcases the ceremony and pageantry of the US Army. Participating units are the 3rd Infantry Regiment, "the Old Guard," and the US Army Band, "Pershing's Own." Additionally, there are the many historical buildings that provide reminders of past events that have occurred on Greenleaf Point. The following chapter provides a look at some of the buildings as they exist today.

It is time to look forward. The previous 100 pages have given a glimpse of the evolution of Fort Lesley J. McNair over two centuries of history. The transformation that occurred upon the arrival of the engineering school suggests that these acres were destined to be a place of learning. The landscape of the post continues to change, though at a slower pace. The National Defense University continues to expand, both in class size and physical facilities. Among the new facilities is Lincoln Hall, an extension alongside Marshall Hall that was dedicated in 2009.

Among the new tenants at the post is the headquarters for the Military District of Washington. In 1942, about five months after the United States entered World War II, the War Department created the US Army Military District of Washington to plan for a ground defense of the nation's capital. MDW was headquartered during those years in temporary buildings at Gravelly Point, Virginia, near Washington National Airport. It moved to Second Street SW in Washington, DC, in the early 1960s, and to its present headquarters at Fort Lesley J. McNair in 1966.

As one walks the acres of this historic US Army post, a continual stream of tributes will be presented—tributes to those who have made significant contributions to improve life, such as Maj. Walter Reed, and who have given their lives, such as Ambassador Chris Stevens. There are many events highlighted earlier in the book that have not only molded Fort Lesley J. McNair into what it is today but also had and may still have an impact on the United States and even the rest of the world.

Now, please turn the page and start the tour.

The above photograph shows the current main gate to Fort Lesley J. McNair. It is a bit more modern than its predecessor, though the Civil War–era cannon tubes are still in place. The below image is a map of the post as it appeared in 2012. (Both, USA.)

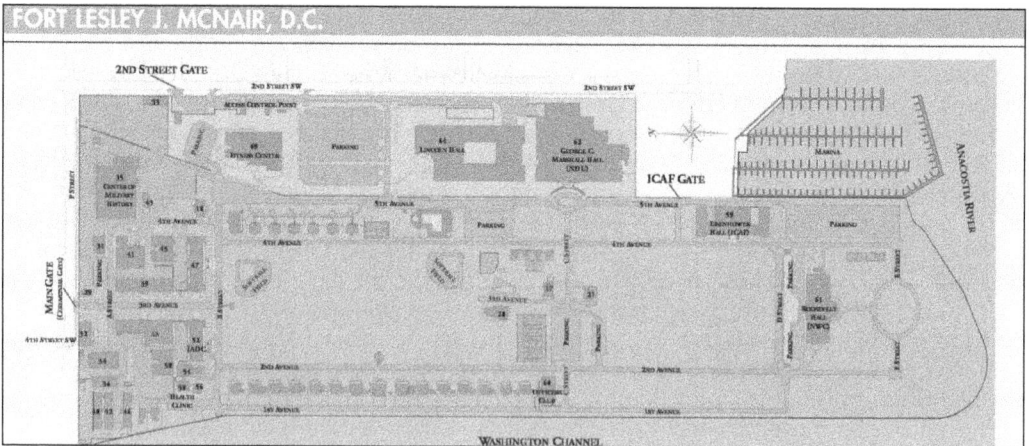

FORT LESLEY J. MCNAIR, D.C.

Marshall Hall, named in honor of Gen. George Catlett Marshall, is the location of the National Defense University. Dedicated in 1992, it is the umbrella organization with all the other colleges underneath. The extensive library, which was once housed at Roosevelt Hall, is now located here. The above photograph is the exterior, and at right is an image of the atrium-like spaciousness that is in the interior. (Both, John Michael.)

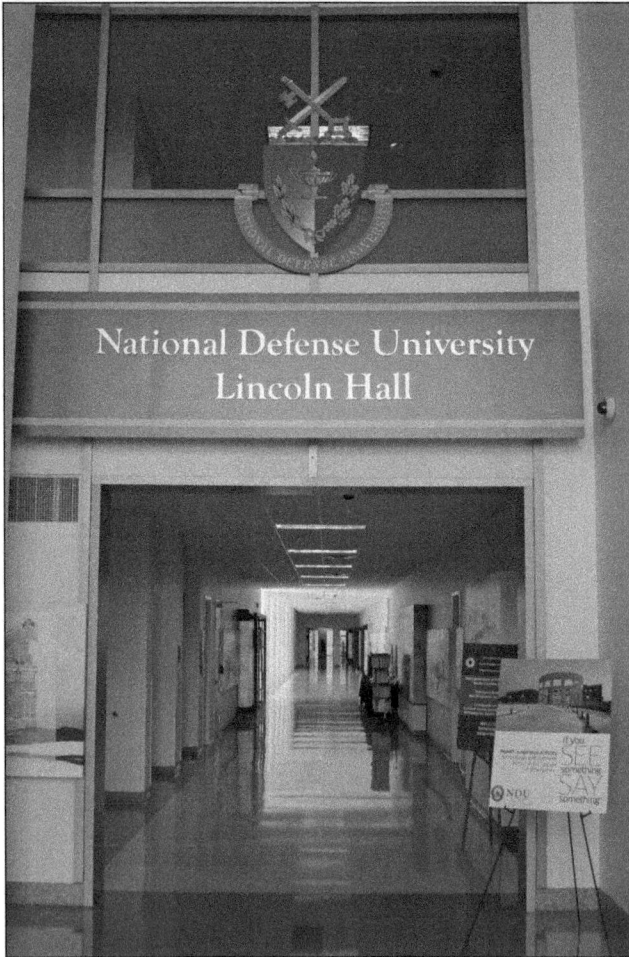

The newest expansion to the National Defense University operation is Lincoln Hall, dedicated to the nation's 16th president, who often visited the acres of Fort McNair when it was Washington Arsenal. It was dedicated in 2009 and provides much-needed expansion with additional office and classroom space. An enclosed corridor/tunnel connects it to Marshall Hall, allowing easy, secure passage between the two buildings. (Both, John Michael.)

Heading south, one encounters a building whose original name is chiseled in stone—Industrial College of the Armed Forces is now the Dwight D. Eisenhower School for National Security and Resource Strategy. It helps graduates develop skills and experience to respond to logistic needs during times of crisis or attack. (Both, John Michael.)

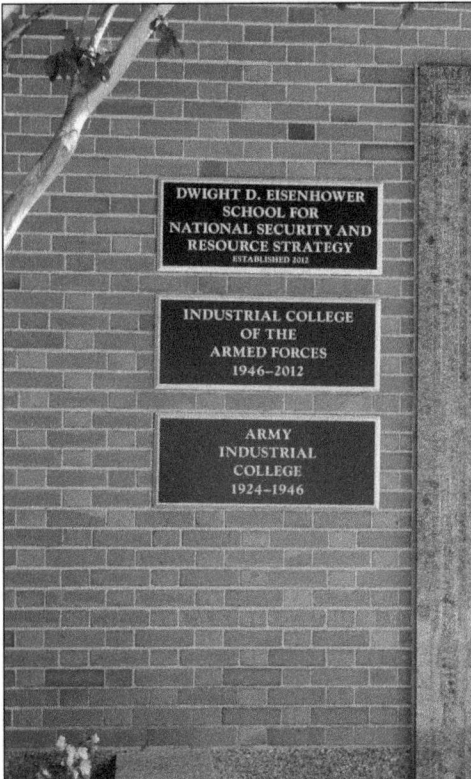

DWIGHT D. EISENHOWER
SCHOOL FOR
NATIONAL SECURITY AND
RESOURCE STRATEGY
ESTABLISHED 2012

INDUSTRIAL COLLEGE
OF THE
ARMED FORCES
1946–2012

ARMY
INDUSTRIAL
COLLEGE
1924–1946

Roosevelt Hall is the next location on this tour. It is a bit southwest, near the end of the peninsula, and it houses the National War College. There are three types of symbols along the steps of the National War College: cannons, anchors, and propellers. They were put in place once the statue of Frederick the Great found a new home at the Army War College at Carlisle Barracks. The symbols suggest that the college serves all branches of the military. (Both, John Michael.)

West of the anchor is an artillery cannon tube—in fact, there are two marking what would be the center of the steps leading to the entrance of the building. The entrance, still as striking as when it was first built over 100 years ago, beckons visitors to enter. (Both, John Michael.)

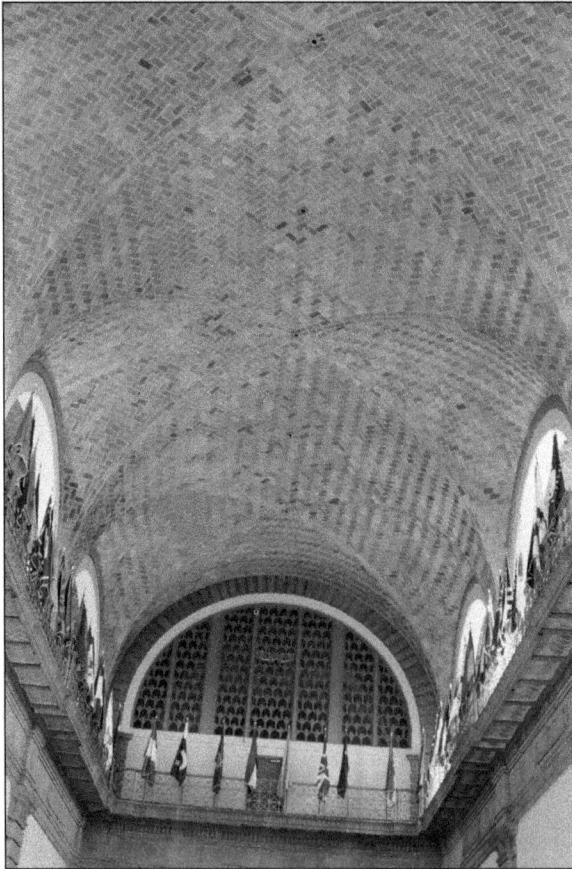

Turning and facing north for a moment, the above photograph shows the expanse of beauty with Grant and Davis Halls in the distance. Upon entrance to Roosevelt Hall, the tendency is to gaze upward to see the pattern in the tiled ceilings bordered by the flags of the states. (Both, John Michael.)

The photograph at right shows George Frost Kennan, an ambassador, diplomat, and author. Fluent in several languages, he was the first deputy commandant of the National War College. The photograph below is a plaque which hangs outside on the wall of the office he once occupied. Kennan wrote and lectured extensively. The results of which became the foundation of US foreign policy, including the Truman Doctrine. He anonymously published "The Sources of Soviet Conduct" under the pen name "X" with the contents suggesting the strategy pursued by the United States during the Cold War. He ultimately was summoned to the State Department to establish a new policy planning staff. (Both, John Michael.)

On the north wall within the commandant's office is a marble tablet with the words "In Memoriam" inscribed with the plaque. Below that is a simple book that is inscribed with names of those who have lost their lives in service to the United States. The book is opened to the page honoring Ambassador Chris Stevens. (Both, John Michael.)

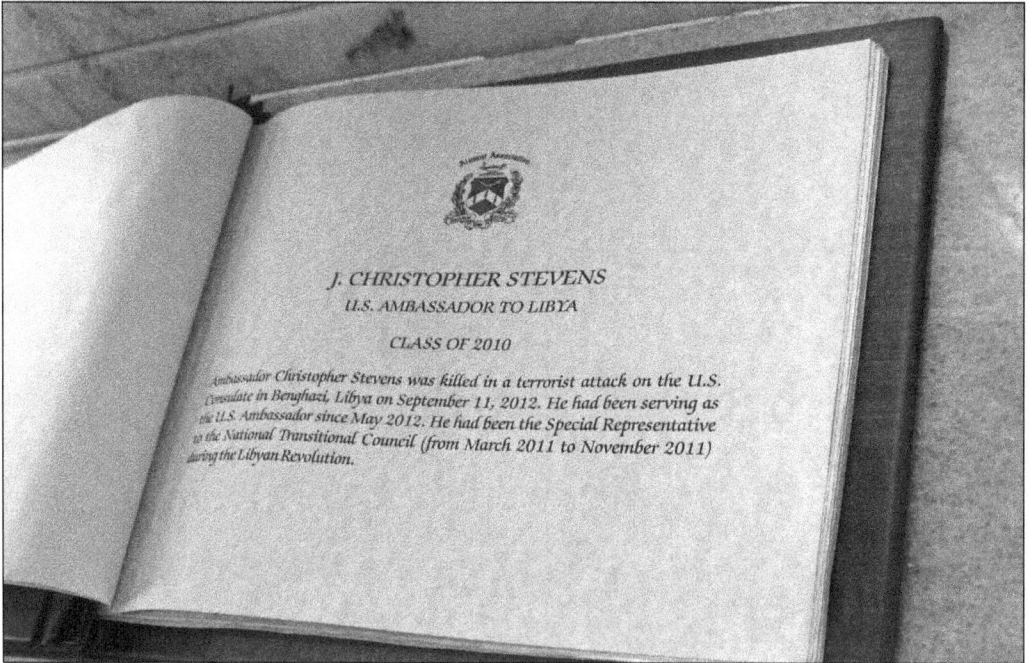

J. CHRISTOPHER STEVENS

U.S. AMBASSADOR TO LIBYA

CLASS OF 2010

Ambassador Christopher Stevens was killed in a terrorist attack on the U.S. Consulate in Benghazi, Libya on September 11, 2012. He had been serving as the U.S. Ambassador since May 2012. He had been the Special Representative to the National Transitional Council (from March 2011 to November 2011) during the Libyan Revolution.

On the way heading northwest, the first building encountered is the majestic officers' club with its Colonial motif. Beyond the club is the long row of officers' quarters, which have been shown elsewhere in this book. (John Michael.)

Due east of the officers' club is Davis Hall, once known as the model arsenal building. Davis Hall is dedicated to Gen. Roy O. Davis, the first African American general officer in the US Army. It is now part of the complex of African studies. (John Michael.)

Heading north again, the above photograph shows Grant Hall, where four Lincoln assassination conspirators, one a woman, were tried and hanged nearby. The plaque on the west side of the building highlights the event and seven weeks of trial that led to it. (Both, John Michael.)

BUILDING 20, GRANT HALL

In 1829, the Federal Penitentiary was built on this site. Designed by Charles Bulfinch, the Architect of the Capitol, the Penitentiary was influenced by the prison reform movement of the 1820's. In 1831, an eastern extension to the building added a women's ward and quarters for the deputy warden. The Deputy Warden's Quarters, is all that remains of the original structures. The center of national attention in 1865, this part of the building became the site for the trial and sentencing of those implicated in the assassination of President Lincoln. Four conspirators were sentenced to death, including the first woman executed by federal order, Mary Surratt. The gallows were constructed in the Penitentiary Courtyard and the executions took place on July 7, 1865.

Continuing north, in nearly the far northwest corner, is building No. 54. It was once the US Army hospital where Maj. Walter Reed practiced medicine, postulated that mosquitoes are the carrier of infectious diseases such as yellow fever, and died while in surgery for appendicitis. The plaque in the photograph below was placed on the 100th anniversary of his death. (Both, John Michael.)

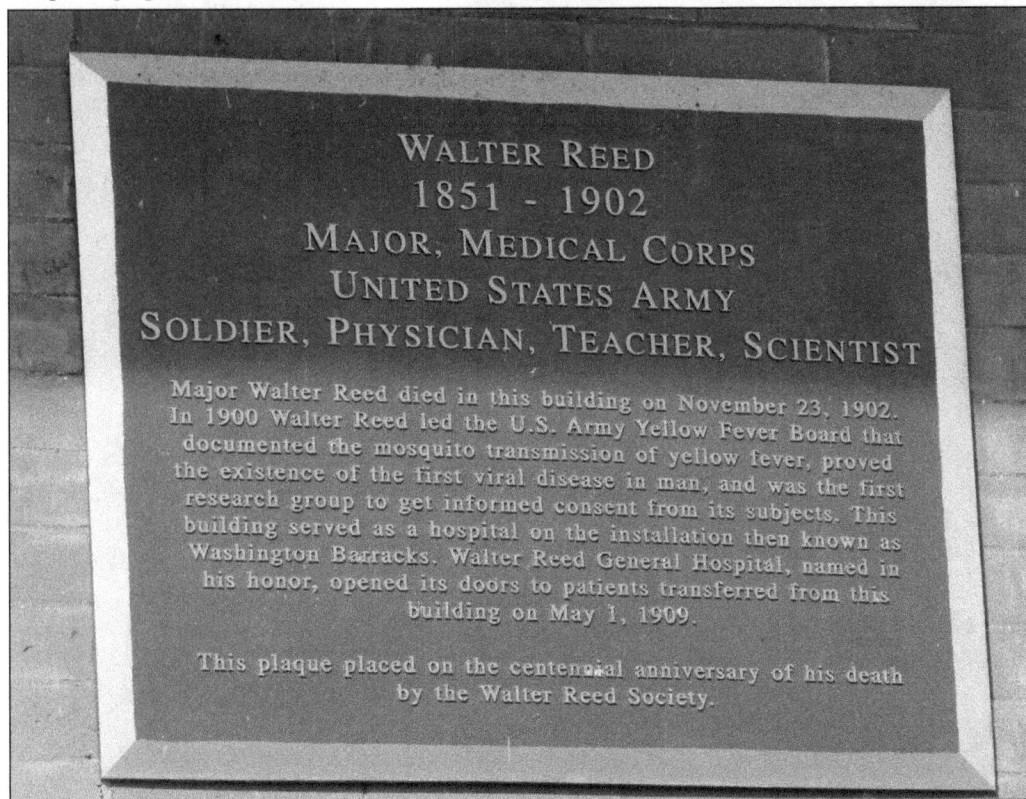

WALTER REED
1851 – 1902
MAJOR, MEDICAL CORPS
UNITED STATES ARMY
SOLDIER, PHYSICIAN, TEACHER, SCIENTIST

Major Walter Reed died in this building on November 23, 1902. In 1900 Walter Reed led the U.S. Army Yellow Fever Board that documented the mosquito transmission of yellow fever, proved the existence of the first viral disease in man, and was the first research group to get informed consent from its subjects. This building served as a hospital on the installation then known as Washington Barracks. Walter Reed General Hospital, named in his honor, opened its doors to patients transferred from this building on May 1, 1909.

This plaque placed on the centennial anniversary of his death by the Walter Reed Society.

The iconic flagpole at the end of the parade field, once hit and split by lightning, is still sporting a two-piece pole with the American colors flying atop proudly in the breeze. At the base is a collection of captured artillery pieces, but gone is the megaphone. Nearby is a baseball or softball field. (John Michael.)

Built with the bricks from the penitentiary, this structure has had many roles. Once, it was the guardhouse. Then, when the engineering school was on post, it was a photography lab. Finally, it became living quarters. It is now one of the three buildings where the daily focus is on African studies. (John Michael.)

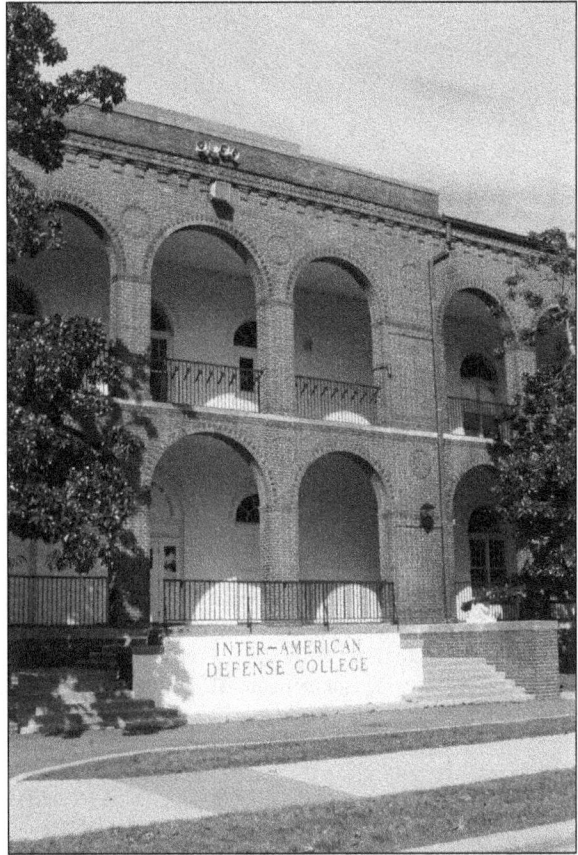

The two enlisted men's barracks now stand with the memories over the decades. Barracks No. 1 housed the music school after the engineers left. Today, it is the Inter-American Defense College headquarters. The larger barracks, No. 2, probably garrisoned the US Army Band. Once the band relocated at Fort Myer, Virginia, Alpha Company from the Old Guard occupied it. It stands empty now, since those soldiers, who are also the "Commander-in-Chief's Guard," are back with the remainder of the US Army's 3rd Infantry Regiment on Fort Myer, Virginia. (Both, John Michael.)

The headquarters of the Military District of Washington is nestled nicely in its building since relocating from the tempo at Gravelly Point in Virginia near National Airport—now Reagan National. ("Tempo" is a military abbreviation for the designation "temporary," whether barracks, headquarters, or other buildings. During World War II and beyond, Washington, DC, was full of tempos, with buildings placed anywhere there was open space.) MDW has taken on more responsibility, as indicated by the sign below, which reads "Joint Force Headquarters–National Capital Region," coordinating the resources of all branches of the military in the Washington, DC, area. (Both, John Michael.)

The gas station was built in 1941. Things were simpler when there were fewer motorized vehicles around. The world seemed to move a little slower but a bit better. The photograph below shows the same site in the 1960s, when the store was expanded. (Above, KBH; below, NARA.)

The above photograph shows a different angle of the same 1960s building, while the photograph below shows the same angle of the structure in 2014. It seems that the only difference is that there are new pumps for the gasoline, which show increasingly higher prices. (Above, NARA; below, John Michael.)

Gone are the movie theater and the commissary; instead, the US Army Center of Military History (CMH) is now a permanent tenant of Fort Lesley J. McNair. CMH does a fine job documenting the history of various units of the US Army. Most recently, it has been made responsible for the history of Arlington National Cemetery, with a dedicated historian assigned to provide in-depth information about those hallowed grounds. (John Michael.)

Looking back in time, here is another view of the historic main gate (the Memorial Gate) with the coastal defense cannon tubes retrieved from the foundry in Richmond, Virginia. This time, the perspective is from the inside of the post looking out. (KBH.)

Visit us at
arcadiapublishing.com